Table of Contents

Meet the...

-ail Word Family
fail, hail, jail, mail, nail, pail, sail, tail, quail, snail, trail 3

-ake Word Family
bake, cake, fake, Jake, lake, make, rake, take, wake, shake, snake 9

-ame Word Family
came, fame, game, lame, name, same, tame, blame, flame, frame, shame 15

-ate Word Family
date, gate, Kate, late, mate, rate, crate, grate, plate, skate, state 21

-ay Word Family
day, hay, jay, say, way, clay, play, spray, stay, sway, tray 27

-eat Word Family
beat, eat, heat, meat, neat, repeat, seat, cheat, pleat, treat, wheat 33

-ee Word Family
agree, bee, Lee, see, flee, free, glee, knee, three, tree 39

-eep Word Family
beep, deep, keep, jeep, weep, creep, sheep, sleep, steep, sweep 45

-eeze Word Family
breeze, freeze, sneeze, squeeze, wheeze 51

-ice Word Family
dice, lice, mice, nice, rice, price, slice, spice, twice 57

-ide Word Family
hide, ride, side, tide, wide, bride, pride, slide, inside, outside 63

-ine Word Family
fine, line, mine, nine, pine, vine, wine, shine, spine, twine, whine 69

-oke Word Family
joke, poke, woke, broke, choke, smoke, spoke, stroke 75

-old Word Family
bold, cold, fold, gold, hold, mold, sold, told, scold 81

-ow Word Family
bow, mow, row, tow, blow, crow, glow, grow, know, slow, snow 87

-y Word Family
cry, dry, fly, fry, shy, sky, spy, try, why, July, butterfly 93

© Evan-Moor Corp. • EMC 3355 • Word Family Stories and Activities

How to Use This Book

The ability to recognize word family patterns is an important part of learning to read. The stories and activities in this book help students increase their reading vocabulary while practicing the essential phonological skills of onset and rime. Each unit follows a consistent format:

Introduce the Word Family

Model blending each initial sound with the word family phoneme. Ask students to point to each picture as they repeat the word after you. Then have students follow the directions to complete the page.

Read the Story

Instruct students to follow along as you read the story aloud. Then have students underline each word family word in the story or poem. Have students read the story again using one of the following methods:

- Read silently
- Echo read
- Choral read

Complete the Activity Pages

The activity pages after each story practice the word family presented and follow a consistent format, leading students to work independently.

Use the Slider

The slider is a quick and easy tool that encourages repeated practice of word family vocabulary, leading to increased oral reading fluency.

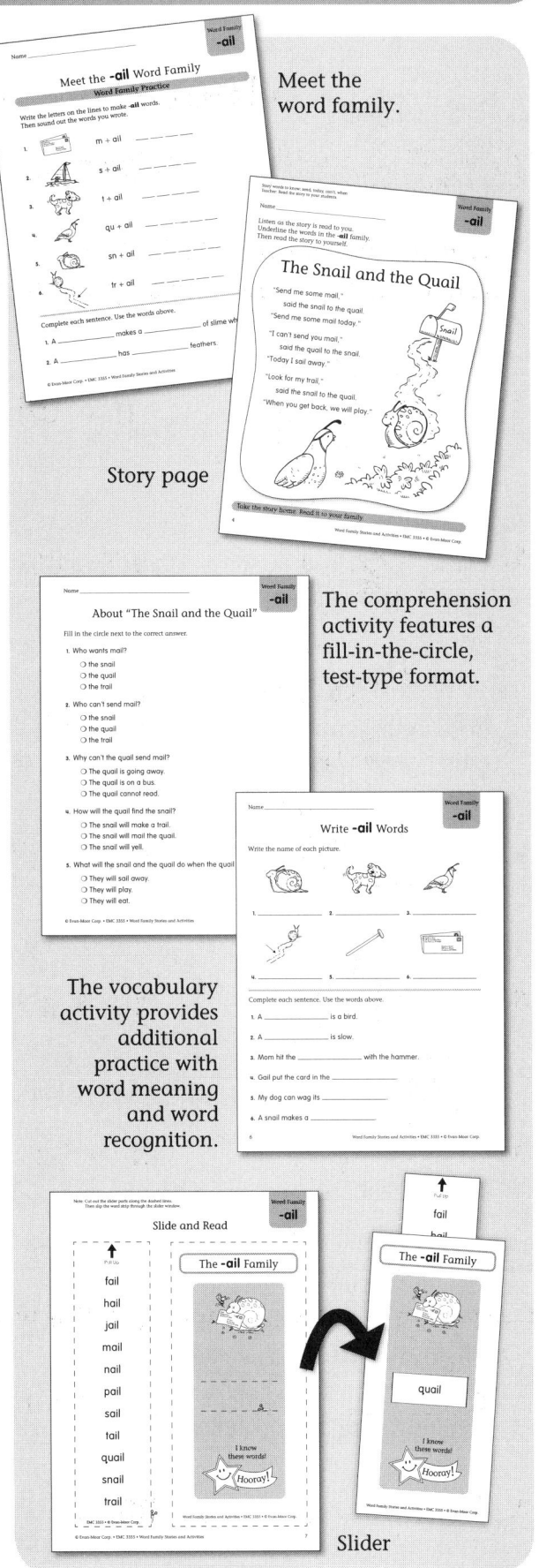

Meet the word family.

Story page

The comprehension activity features a fill-in-the-circle, test-type format.

The vocabulary activity provides additional practice with word meaning and word recognition.

Slider

Name_____

Word Family -ail

Meet the -ail Word Family

Word Family Practice

Write the letters on the lines to make **-ail** words.
Then sound out the words you wrote.

1.    m + ail   __ __ __ __

2.    s + ail   __ __ __

3.    t + ail   __ __ __

4.    qu + ail   __ __ __ __ __

5.    sn + ail   __ __ __ __

6.   tr + ail   __ __ __ __

Complete each sentence. Use the words above.

1. A _____ makes a _____ of slime when it moves.

2. A _____ has _____ feathers.

© Evan-Moor Corp. • EMC 3355 • Word Family Stories and Activities

Story words to know: send, today, can't, when
Teacher: Read the story to your students.

Word Family -ail

Name _____

Listen as the story is read to you.
Underline the words in the **-ail** family.
Then read the story to yourself.

The Snail and the Quail

"Send me some mail,"
  said the snail to the quail.
"Send me some mail today."

"I can't send you mail,"
  said the quail to the snail.
"Today I sail away."

"Look for my trail,"
  said the snail to the quail.
"When you get back, we will play."

Take the story home. Read it to your family.

Word Family Stories and Activities • EMC 3355 • © Evan-Moor Corp.

Name_____

Word Family -ail

About "The Snail and the Quail"

Fill in the circle next to the correct answer.

1. Who wants mail?

    ○ the snail
    ○ the quail
    ○ the trail

2. Who can't send mail?

    ○ the snail
    ○ the quail
    ○ the trail

3. Why can't the quail send mail?

    ○ The quail is going away.
    ○ The quail is on a bus.
    ○ The quail cannot read.

4. How will the quail find the snail?

    ○ The snail will make a trail.
    ○ The snail will mail the quail.
    ○ The snail will yell.

5. What will the snail and the quail do when the quail gets back?

    ○ They will sail away.
    ○ They will play.
    ○ They will eat.

Name _____

Write -ail Words

Word Family -ail

Write the name of each picture.

1. _____   2. _____   3. _____

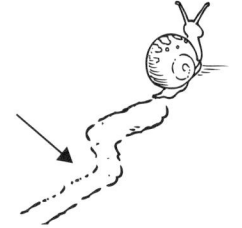
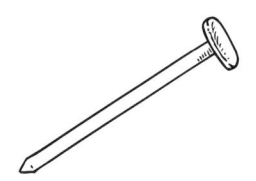

4. _____   5. _____   6. _____

Complete each sentence. Use the words above.

1. A _____ is a bird.

2. A _____ is slow.

3. Mom hit the _____ with the hammer.

4. Gail put the card in the _____.

5. My dog can wag its _____.

6. A snail makes a _____.

Note: Cut out the slider parts along the dashed lines.
Then slip the word strip through the slider window.

Word Family -ail

Slide and Read

↑ Pull Up

fail

hail

jail

mail

nail

pail

sail

tail

quail

snail

trail

The -ail Family

I know these words! Hooray!

end of -ail family

Name _____

Word Family
-ake

Meet the -ake Word Family

Word Family Practice

Write the letters on the lines to make **-ake** words.
Then sound out the words you wrote.

1.  J + ake ___ ___ ___ ___

2. 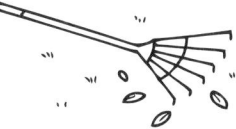 l + ake ___ ___ ___ ___

3.  r + ake ___ ___ ___ ___

4.  sh + ake ___ ___ ___ ___ ___

5.  sn + ake ___ ___ ___ ___ ___

6.  f + ake ___ ___ ___ ___

Complete each sentence. Use the words above.

1. A _____ is a garden tool.

2. A _____ has a long body and no legs.

3. Look at the boat on the _____.

Story words to know: pushes, across, 'round, pulls, grass
Teacher: Read the story to your students.

Word Family -ake

Name _____

Listen as the story is read to you.
Underline the words in the **-ake** family.
Then read the story to yourself.

The Fake Rake

Dad asks Jake to rake.

Jake gives the rake a shake.
In and out. In and out.
Ssss. The rake is now a snake.

Jake pushes the rake.
Up and back. Up and back.
The rake takes Jake across a lake.

Jake uses the rake to mix.
'Round and 'round. 'Round and 'round.
Jake makes a cake.

Then Jake pulls the rake in the grass.
Now the rake is just a rake.

Take the story home. Read it to your family.

Name_____

Word Family -ake

About "The Fake Rake"

Circle a Beginning, Middle, and End sentence to retell the story.

Beginning
1. Dad asks Jake to rake.
2. Dad asks Jake to bake.
3. Dad asks Jake to play.

Middle
1. Jake rakes.
2. Jake runs.
3. Jake plays make-believe.

End
1. Jake rakes.
2. Jake makes a cake.
3. Jake goes on a lake.

Fill in the circle next to **yes** or **no**.

1. The rake is a real snake.
   - ○ yes
   - ○ no

2. Jake likes make-believe.
   - ○ yes
   - ○ no

3. Jake rakes the grass.
   - ○ yes
   - ○ no

Name_____

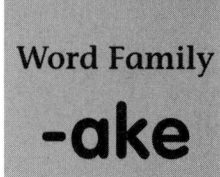

Write -ake Words

Write the name of each picture.

1. _____ 2. _____ 3. _____

Complete each sentence. Use the words below.

> bake   cake   fake   lake   shake

1. Fish swim in the _____.

2. The dog can _____ its paw.

3. I like to eat _____.

4. Cam will _____ a white cake.

5. The snake is not real. It is _____.

Note: Cut out the slider parts along the dashed lines.
Then slip the word strip through the slider window.

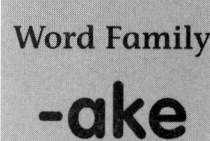

Slide and Read

↑ Pull Up

bake

cake

fake

Jake

lake

make

rake

take

wake

shake

snake

The -ake Family

I know these words!

Hooray!

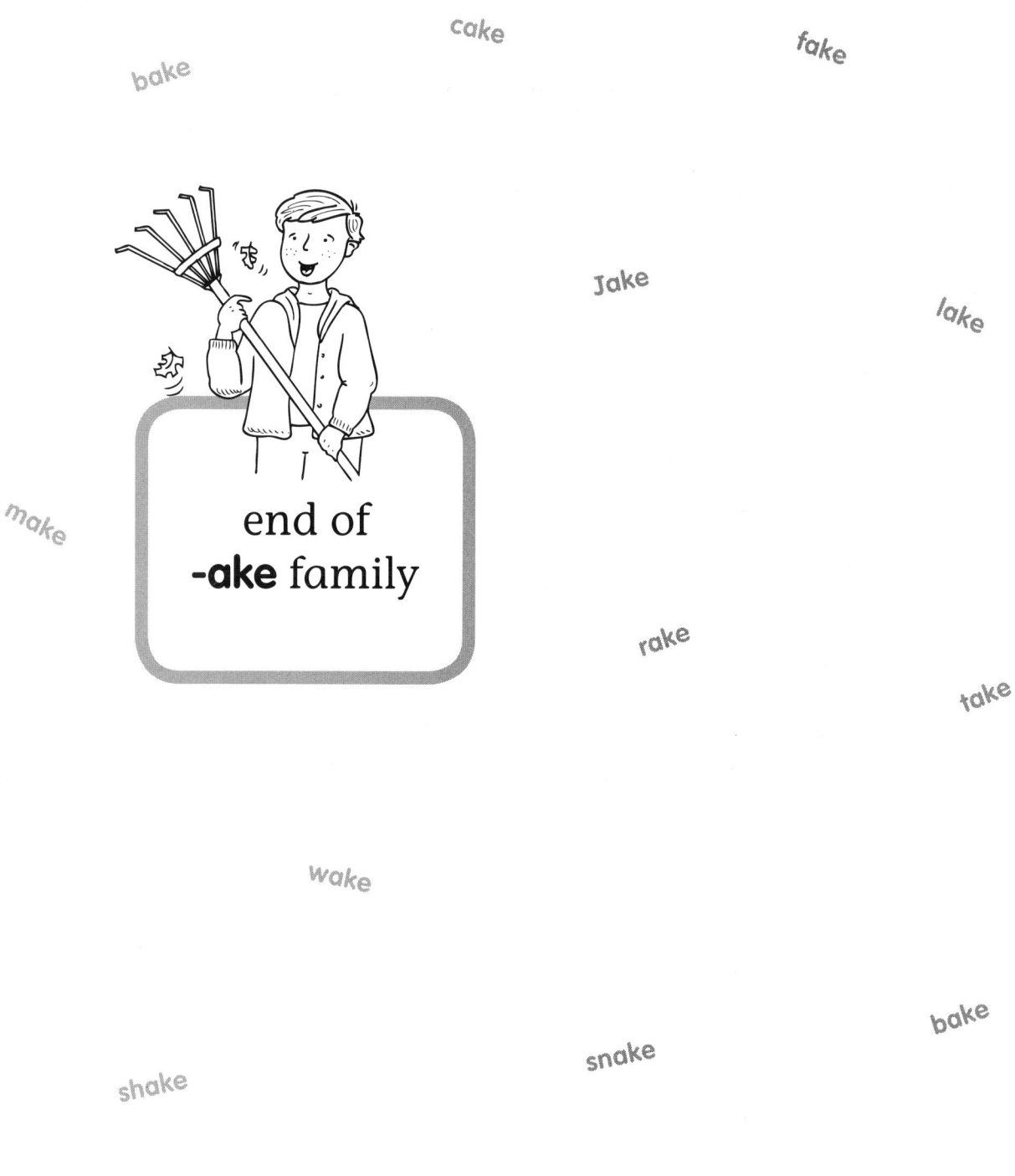

Name _____

Word Family
-ame

Meet the -ame Word Family

Word Family Practice

Write the letters on the lines to make **-ame** words.
Then sound out the words you wrote.

1.    g + ame   __ __ __ __

2.    s + ame   __ __ __ __

3.    t + ame   __ __ __ __

4.    fl + ame   __ __ __ __ __

5.    fr + ame   __ __ __ __ __

Read these **-ame** words.

came   lame   shame

Complete each sentence. Use the words above.

1. We can play my new computer _____.

2. A lion is wild, not _____.

3. My art hangs in a _____.

© Evan-Moor Corp. • EMC 3355 • Word Family Stories and Activities

Story words to know: never, bears, brave, fire, draws
Teacher: Read the story to your students.

Word Family
-ame

Name _____

Listen as the story is read to you.
Underline the words in the **-ame** family.
Then read the story to yourself.

The Game

Every day, James makes up a game.
The game is never the same.

James sees bears.
James is brave.
He can tame them.

James hears a boom.
He sees a flame!
He puts out the fire.

James draws.
He uses many colors.
James puts his art in a big frame.

James plays fun games.

Take the story home. Read it to your family.

Name _____

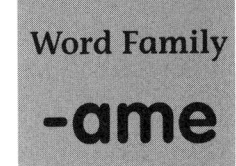

About "The Game"

Fill in the circle next to the correct answer.

1. What is the story about?

    ○ James sings.
    ○ James makes up games.
    ○ James does not like to play games.

2. What does James do to the bears?

    ○ James names the bears.
    ○ James feeds the bears.
    ○ James tames the bears.

3. James sees a flame. He _____.

    ○ watches the fire
    ○ puts out the fire
    ○ puts a log on the fire

4. Where does James put his art?

    ○ in a box
    ○ in a frame
    ○ on the wall

5. Which one tells about James?

    ○ James is old.
    ○ James is sad.
    ○ James is fun.

Write -ame Words

Word Family -ame

Write the name of each picture.

1. _____ 2. _____ 3. _____

Complete each sentence. Use the words below.

blame   came   flame   tame

1. James _____ to see me.

2. I will _____ my pet tiger.

3. The _____ is hot.

4. I will take the _____ for this mess.

Write a sentence about a game you play. Use the word **game**.

_____
_____
_____.

Note: Cut out the slider parts along the dashed lines. Then slip the word strip through the slider window.

Word Family

-ame

Slide and Read

↑
Pull Up

came

fame

game

lame

name

same

tame

blame

flame

frame

shame

The **-ame** Family

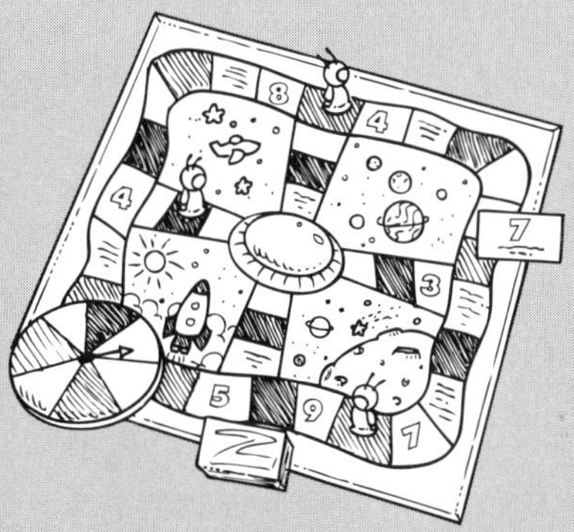

I know these words!

Hooray!

came
fame
game
lame
name 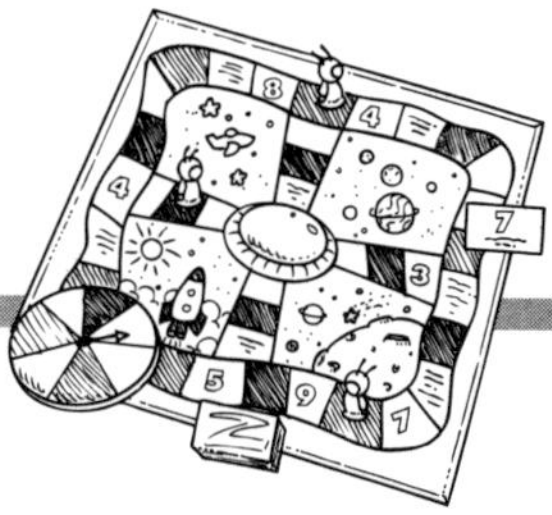
same
end of
-ame family
tame
blame
frame
flame
shame
came
fame
game
lame

Name _____

Word Family
-ate

Meet the **-ate** Word Family

Word Family Practice

Write the letters on the lines to make **-ate** words.
Then sound out the words you wrote.

1. 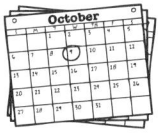 d + ate   ___ ___ ___ ___

2.  g + ate   ___ ___ ___ ___

3.  K + ate   ___ ___ ___ ___

4.  l + ate   ___ ___ ___ ___

5.  pl + ate   ___ ___ ___ ___ ___

6.  sk + ate   ___ ___ ___ ___ ___

Complete each sentence. Use the words above.

1. Dad put the meat on a large round _____.

2. The fence around my house has a _____.

3. Kate likes to _____ on the icy pond.

© Evan-Moor Corp. • EMC 3355 • Word Family Stories and Activities

Story words to know: icy, great, pond, smooth, dinner
Teacher: Read the story to your students.

Word Family -ate

Name _____

Listen as the story is read to you.
Underline the words in the **-ate** family.
Then read the story to yourself.

Skate

The day is cold.
The day is icy.
"What a great day!" says Kate.

She runs down the path.
Kate sees her friend at the gate.
She isn't too late for the fun.

The pond shines.
It looks as smooth as a dinner plate.
Kate pushes off.
Around and around she begins to skate.

Take the story home. Read it to your family.

Name _____

Word Family -ate

About "Skate"

Fill in the circle next to **yes** or **no**.

1. It is too cold to skate.

   ○ yes　　　○ no

2. It is a great day to swim.

   ○ yes　　　○ no

3. The pond is as smooth as a dinner plate.

   ○ yes　　　○ no

4. The pond is icy.

   ○ yes　　　○ no

5. Kate can skate.

   ○ yes　　　○ no

Draw a line to make a match.

1. 　　　• 　　　• Kate can skate.

2. 　　　• 　　　• Kate sees her friend at the gate.

3. 　　　• 　　　• Kate runs down the path.

© Evan-Moor Corp. • EMC 3355 • Word Family Stories and Activities

Name _____

Word Family
-ate

Write **-ate** Words

Write the name of each picture.

1. _____   2. _____   3. _____

Complete each sentence. Use the words below.

> crate   date   gate   late   plate

1. I ran fast so I would not be _____.

2. The garden has a _____.

3. Mom put the cake on a paper _____.

4. The apples are in a _____.

5. What is the _____ today?

24   Word Family Stories and Activities • EMC 3355 • © Evan-Moor Corp.

Note: Cut out the slider parts along the dashed lines. Then slip the word strip through the slider window.

Slide and Read

Word Family -ate

↑ Pull Up

date

gate

Kate

late

mate

rate

crate

grate

plate

skate

state

The **-ate** Family

I know these words! Hooray!

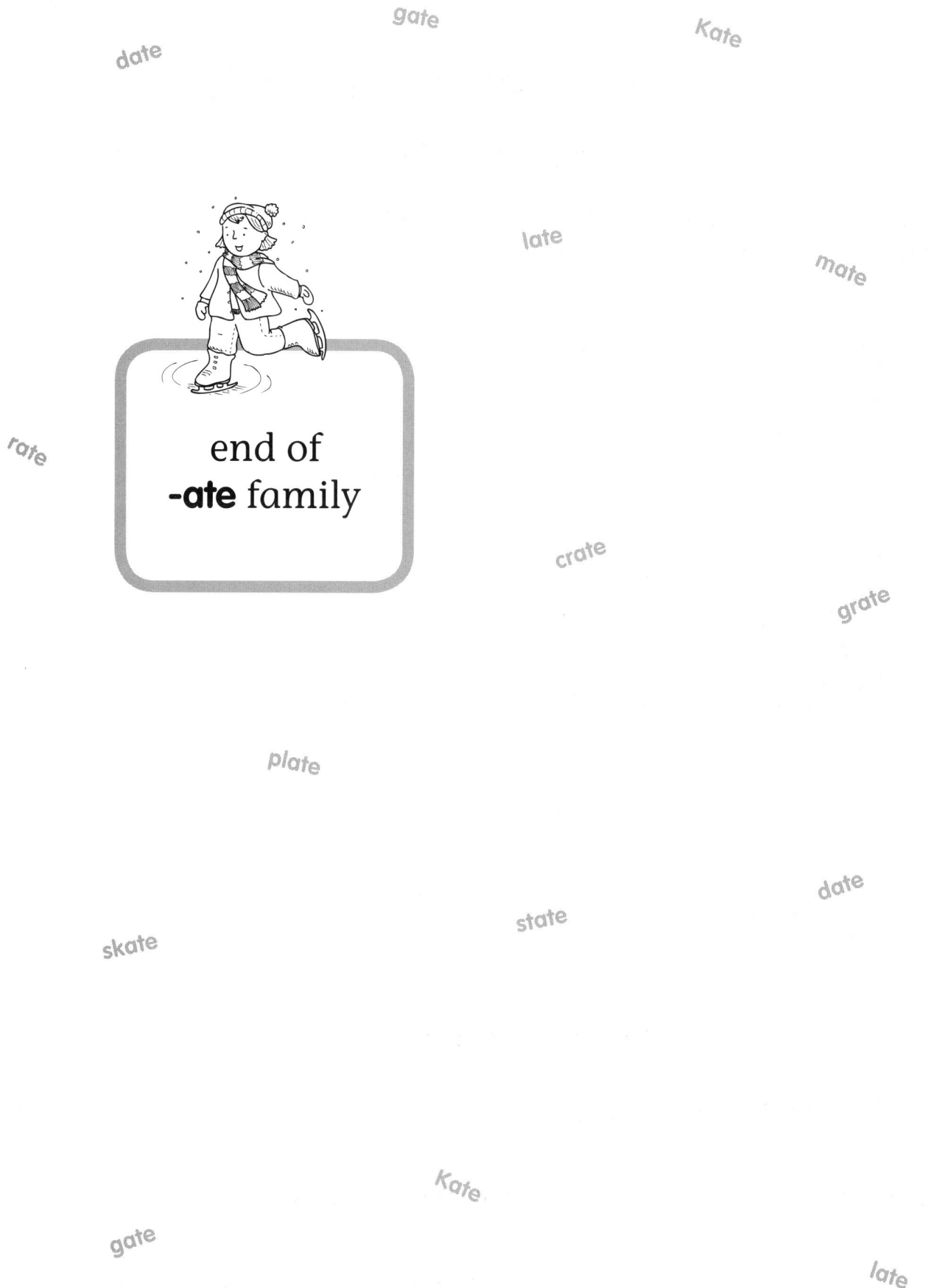

Name _____

Word Family
-ay

Meet the -ay Word Family

Word Family Practice

Write the letters on the lines to make -**ay** words.
Then sound out the words you made.

1.   j + ay   ___ ___ ___

2.  h + ay   ___ ___ ___

3.  cl + ay   ___ ___ ___ ___

4.  pl + ay   ___ ___ ___ ___

5.  sw + ay   ___ ___ ___ ___

6.  spr + ay   ___ ___ ___ ___ ___

Complete each sentence. Use the words above.

1. My horse eats dry grass, or _____.

2. I like to _____ music while I draw.

3. Can you _____ the flowers with the garden hose?

Story words to know: hose, crayons, form, music, barn
Teacher: Read the story to your students.

Word Family
-ay

Name _____

Listen as the story is read to you.
Underline the words in the **-ay** family.
Then read the story to yourself.

A Day of Fun

Come this way.
Have some fun!
Spray with a hose.
Run in the sun.

Get some crayons.
Take some clay.
Make a drawing.
Form a blue jay.

Play some music.
Sing and sway.
Find the red barn.
Jump in the hay.

What do you say?
You want to stay.
Hip, hip, hooray!

Take the story home. Read it to your family.

Name _____

Word Family

-ay

About "A Day of Fun"

Write and circle what you can do on a fun day.

1. Form a blue jay with _____.   gray   clay

2. Jump in the _____.   hay   ham

3. Use a hose to _____.   stay   spray

4. _____ some music.   Play   Pull

5. Dance and _____ to the music.   sway   swim

Fill in the circle next to the correct answer.

1. What is a good name for the story?
   ○ The Sad Day
   ○ A Day to Play

2. Where is the hay?
   ○ in the barn
   ○ on a tray

3. What is a word that means you are **happy**?
   ○ hooray
   ○ boo

© Evan-Moor Corp. • EMC 3355 • Word Family Stories and Activities

Name _____

Word Family
-ay

Write -ay Words

Fill in the circle next to the name of each picture.

1.
   - ○ ham
   - ○ may
   - ○ hay

2.
   - ○ clay
   - ○ day
   - ○ spray

3.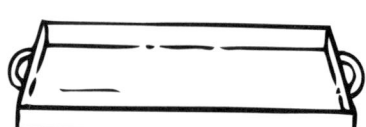
   - ○ they
   - ○ tray
   - ○ the

Complete each sentence. Use the words below.

> gray   play   say   Today   way

1. Matt likes to _____ tag.

2. The sky is _____ when it rains.

3. He will show me the _____ to the barn.

4. I hope Mom will _____ yes.

5. _____ is a fun day.

Note: Cut out the slider parts along the dashed lines.
Then slip the word strip through the slider window.

Word Family -ay

Slide and Read

The -ay Family

↑ Pull Up

day

hay

jay

say

way

clay

play

spray

stay

sway

tray

I know these words! Hooray!

day · hay · jay · say · way · clay · end of -ay family · play · spray · stay · day · sway · tray · jay · hay · say

Name_____

Word Family
-eat

Meet the -eat Word Family

Word Family Practice

Write the letters on the lines to make -**eat** words.
Then sound out the words you made.

1.  b + eat ___ ___ ___ ___

2.  m + eat ___ ___ ___ ___

3.  h + eat ___ ___ ___ ___

4.  tr + eat ___ ___ ___ ___ ___

5.  wh + eat ___ ___ ___ ___ ___

Complete each sentence. Use the words above.

1. Will you please turn up the _____?

2. After dinner, I want a _____.

3. Dad will _____ the eggs and milk.

4. That bread is made from _____.

Story words to know: eggs, stir, bake, yummy
Teacher: Read the story to your students.

Word Family
-eat

Name _____

Listen as the story is read to you.
Underline the words in the **-eat** family.
Then read the story to yourself.

Eat a Treat!

I want to eat a treat.

First, I put in two eggs and I beat.

I beat my treat.

Next, I add wheat and I stir.

I stir my treat.

Then, I turn on the heat.

I bake my treat.

Last, it is ready to eat.

I eat my treat.

Mmmm...a treat is yummy to eat!

Take the story home. Read it to your family.

Name _____

Word Family
-eat

About "Eat a Treat!"

Fill in the circle next to the correct answer.

1. What is the story about?
   - ○ reading a book
   - ○ making a treat
   - ○ walking a dog

2. What did the story say to do first when you make a treat?
   - ○ add wheat and stir
   - ○ turn on the heat
   - ○ put in two eggs and beat

3. What is the treat?
   - ○ a muffin
   - ○ a banana
   - ○ eggs and milk

Draw a line to make a match.

1.  •   • I turn on the heat.

2.  •   • I eat my treat.

3.  •   • I put in two eggs and beat.

Name _____

Write -eat Words

Fill in the circle next to the name of each picture.

1.

    ○ meat
    ○ mean
    ○ seat

2.

    ○ where
    ○ wheat
    ○ meat

3.

    ○ bear
    ○ beat
    ○ neat

Complete each sentence. Use the words below.

> heat   neat   repeat   seat   treat

1. The sun gives off _____.

2. Can I sit in the front _____?

3. A cookie is a yummy _____.

4. She keeps her room _____.

5. Please _____ what you said.

Note: Cut out the slider parts along the dashed lines. Then slip the word strip through the slider window.

Word Family -eat

Slide and Read

Pull Up

beat

eat

heat

meat

neat

repeat

seat

cheat

pleat

treat

wheat

The **-eat** Family

I know these words!

Hooray!

beat eat heat

meat neat

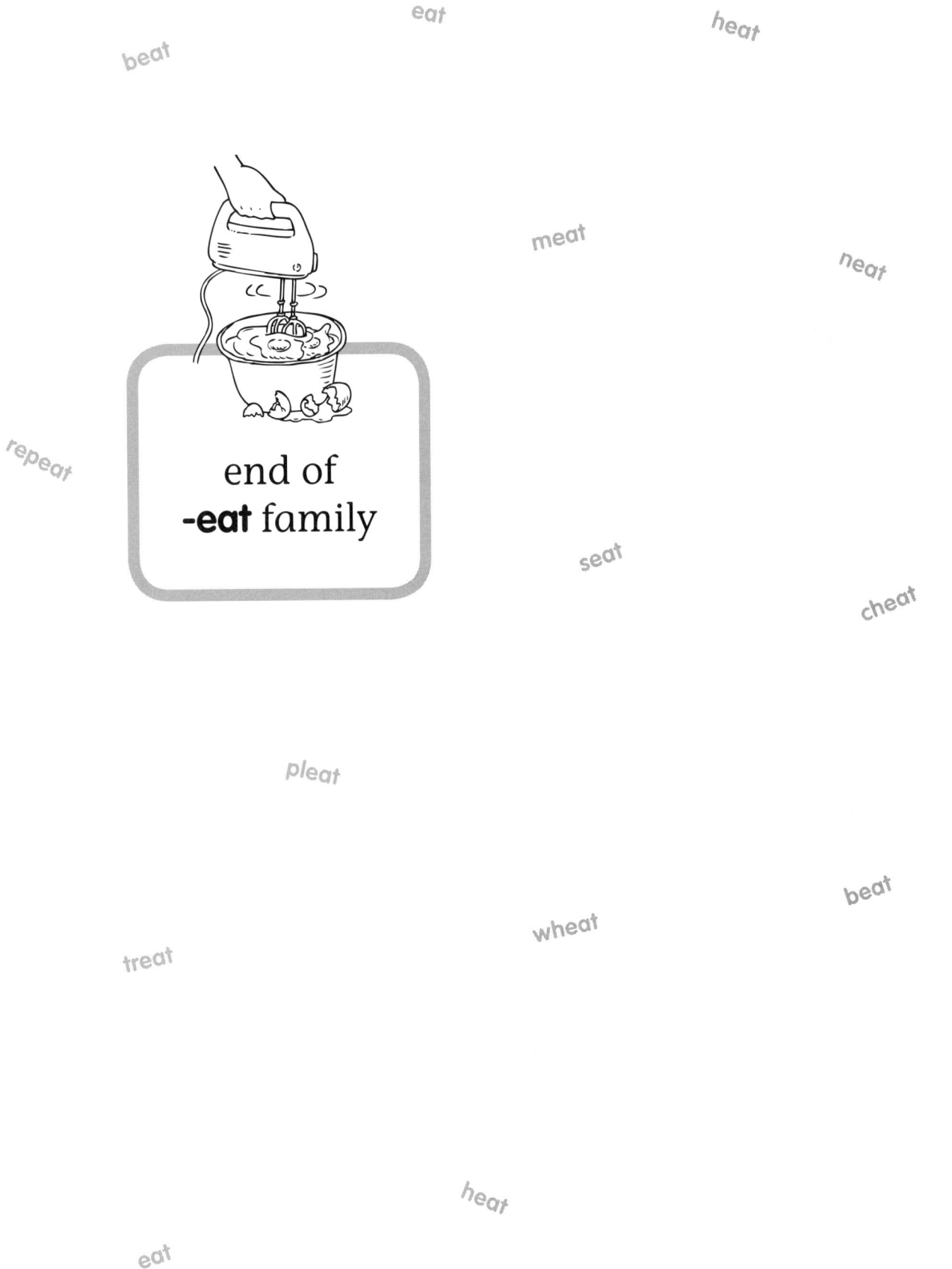

end of -eat family

repeat seat cheat

pleat

treat wheat beat

heat

eat meat

Name _____

Word Family
-ee

Meet the -ee Word Family

Word Family Practice

Write the letters on the lines to make -ee words.
Then sound out the words you made.

1.  b + ee   ___ ___ ___

2.  fr + ee   ___ ___ ___ ___

3.  gl + ee   ___ ___ ___ ___

4.  kn + ee   ___ ___ ___ ___

5.  tr + ee   ___ ___ ___ ___

6.  thr + ee   ___ ___ ___ ___ ___

Complete each sentence. Use the words above.

1. Your _____ is part of your leg.

2. Jay picks apples from that _____.

3. A honey_____ has four wings.

© Evan-Moor Corp. • EMC 3355 • Word Family Stories and Activities

Story words to know: pal, close, together, honey
Teacher: Read the story to your students.

Word Family -ee

Name _____

Listen as the story is read to you.
Underline the words in the **-ee** family.
Then read the story to yourself.

You and Me

You are my pal.

We're as close as can be.

We go together

like honey and a bee,

like a leg and a knee,

like a bird and a tree,

like one, two, three!

Don't you agree?

Take the story home. Read it to your family.

Name_____

Word Family -ee

About "You and Me"

Draw a line to make a match.

1.  • • tree

2. **one, two,** • • knee

3. 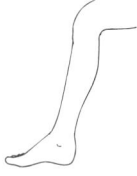 • • bee

4.  • • three

---

Fill in the circle next to **yes** or **no**.

1. The story is about friends.

   ○ yes   ○ no

2. The friends like each other.

   ○ yes   ○ no

The word **glee** means "a feeling of joy."
Trace the word **glee**. Complete the sentence with the name of a friend.

My friend _____ makes me laugh with glee.

Name _____

Word Family
-ee

Write -ee Words

Write the name of each picture.

1. _____ 2. _____ 3. _____

Complete each sentence. Use the words below.

> agree   free   knee   see   three

1. I can bend my _____.

2. What do you _____ in the tree?

3. I _____ with what you said.

4. I see _____ bees on the flower.

5. You do not have to pay. The game is _____.

42   Word Family Stories and Activities • EMC 3355 • © Evan-Moor Corp.

Note: Cut out the slider parts along the dashed lines. Then slip the word strip through the slider window.

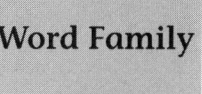

Slide and Read

The -ee Family

↑ Pull Up

agree

bee

Lee

see

flee

free

glee

knee

three

tree

I know these words!
Hooray!

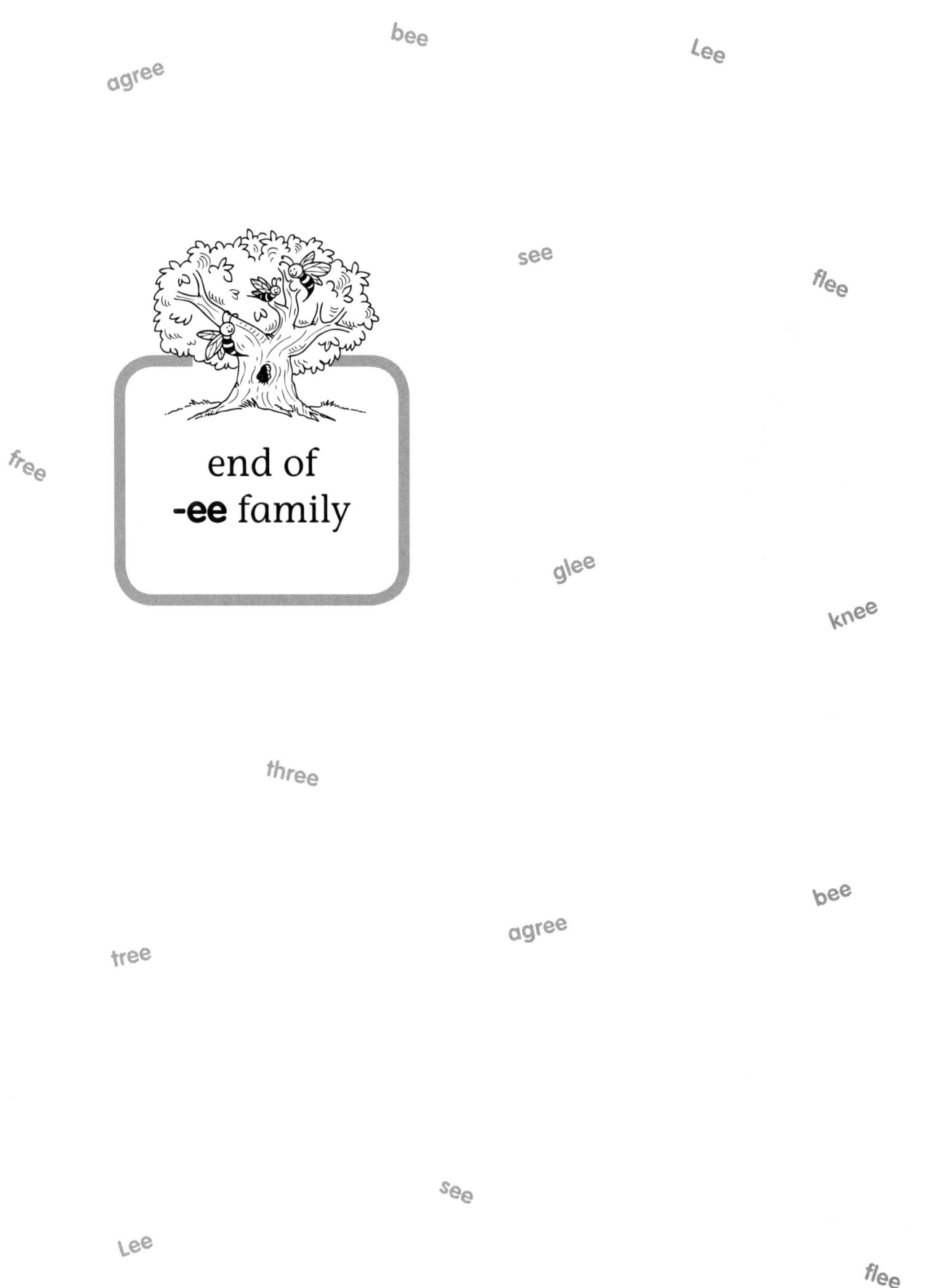

Name_____

Word Family
-eep

Meet the -eep Word Family

Word Family Practice

Write the letters on the lines to make -**eep** words.
Then sound out the words you made.

1.  d + eep ___ ___ ___ ___

2.  cr + eep ___ ___ ___ ___ ___

3.  sh + eep ___ ___ ___ ___ ___

4.  sl + eep ___ ___ ___ ___ ___

5.  st + eep ___ ___ ___ ___ ___

Read these -**eep** words.

keep   weep   beep

Complete each sentence. Use the words above.

1. That lake is very _____.

2. The hill is too _____ for me to go up.

3. The dog likes to _____ low to the ground.

Story words to know: ready, job, around, safe
Teacher: Read the story to your students.

Word Family -eep

Name _____

Listen as the story is read to you.
Underline the words in the **-eep** family.
Then read the story to yourself.

Who Cares for Sheep?

The dog is not ready to sleep.

He has a job.

He cares for sheep.

The dog can creep low.

He can run around the sheep.

He makes them stay in the grass.

The sheep stay away from steep land.

They will not go into deep water.

The dog will keep the sheep safe.

Take the story home. Read it to your family.

Name_____

Word Family -eep

About "Who Cares for Sheep?"

Fill in the circle next to the correct answer.

1. What is the story about?

    ○ a dog and cat
    ○ sheep
    ○ a dog and sheep

2. Where is a good place for sheep?

    ○ in deep water
    ○ on steep land
    ○ in grass

3. What do sheep eat?

    ○ grass
    ○ land
    ○ dogs

Draw a line to make a match.

1. •   • The dog keeps the sheep safe.

2. •   • The sheep eat grass.

3. •   • The dog can creep.

© Evan-Moor Corp. • EMC 3355 • Word Family Stories and Activities

Name_____

Word Family
-eep

Write **-eep** Words

Write the name of each picture.

1. _____ 2. _____ 3. _____

4. _____ 5. _____ 6. _____

Complete each sentence. Use the words below.

> deep   keep   sheep   sweep

1. The dog cares for the _____.

2. Mom and Dad _____ me safe.

3. Jen will _____ away the dirt.

4. Jon does not swim in _____ water.

Note: Cut out the slider parts along the dashed lines.
Then slip the word strip through the slider window.

Word Family -eep

Slide and Read

↑ Pull Up

beep

deep

keep

jeep

weep

creep

sheep

sleep

steep

sweep

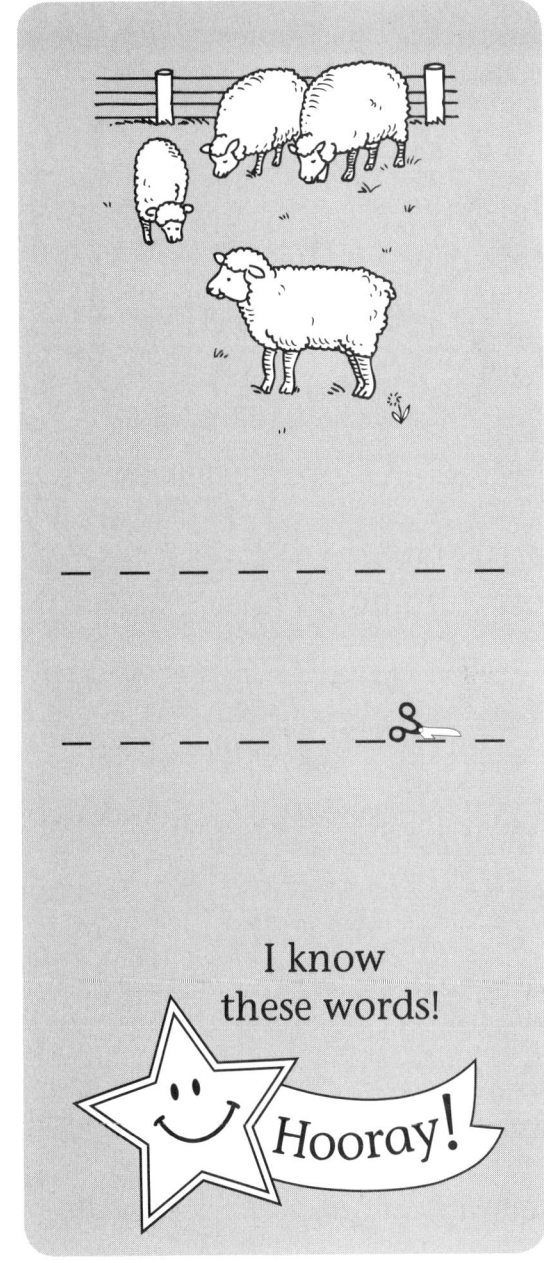

The **-eep** Family

I know these words! Hooray!

beep deep keep

jeep weep

creep

end of
-eep family

sheep

sleep

steep

sweep beep deep

jeep

keep weep

Name _____

Word Family
-eeze

Meet the **-eeze** Word Family

Word Family Practice

Write the letters on the lines to make **-eeze** words.
Then sound out the words you wrote.

1. br + eeze ___ ___ ___ ___ ___

2.  fr + eeze ___ ___ ___ ___ ___

3. 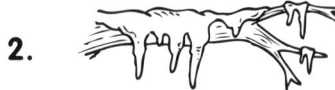 sn + eeze ___ ___ ___ ___ ___

4.  squ + eeze ___ ___ ___ ___ ___ ___

Read these **-eeze** words.

wheeze   tweeze

Complete each sentence. Use the words above.

1. Cold air makes water _____ into ice.

2. The _____ blew the trees.

3. I _____ when it is hard to breathe.

4. Please cover your mouth when you _____.

Story words to know: lettuce, carrots, peppers, tomato, salad
Teacher: Read the story to your students.

Word Family -eeze

Name _____

Listen as the story is read to you.
Underline the words in the **-eeze** family.
Then read the story to yourself.

Squeeze, Squeeze, Squeeze

You toss the lettuce

with carrots  and cheese .

But…

Don't put in peppers  or I'll sneeze, sneeze, sneeze.

Skip the cold tomato or I'll freeze, freeze, freeze.

Don't put in peanuts  or I'll wheeze, wheeze, wheeze.

Just add some lemon

with a squeeze, squeeze, squeeze.

I bet this salad will be sure to please!

Take the story home. Read it to your family.

Name _____

Word Family
-eeze

About
"Squeeze, Squeeze, Squeeze"

Complete each sentence.

1.  make the boy _____.

2. 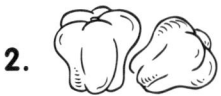 make the boy _____.

3. A cold 🍊 makes the boy _____.

Make each sound. Draw a line to match the sounds to the words.

1. Achoo! •   • squeeze

2. Brrrr! •   • sneeze

3. Ouch!   •   • freeze

Draw two things you can squeeze.

Name _____

Word Family
-eeze

Write **-eeze** Words

Complete each sentence. Use the words below.

> breeze   freeze   sneeze   squeeze

1. I will _____ the lemon.

2. Water can _____ into ice.

3. I _____ when I have a cold.

4. A _____ is a soft wind.

Write a sentence about a soft wind. Use the word **breeze**.

_____

_____.

Write a sentence about something that gets cold. Use the word **freeze**.

_____

_____.

Note: Cut out the slider parts along the dashed lines. Then slip the word strip through the slider window.

Word Family -eeze

Slide and Read

↑ Pull Up

breeze

freeze

sneeze

squeeze

wheeze

The **-eeze** Family

I know these words! Hooray!

end of
-eeze family

Name_____

Word Family -ice

Meet the -ice Word Family

Word Family Practice

Write the letters on the lines to make -ice words.
Then sound out the words you wrote.

1.  d + ice   ___ ___ ___ ___

2.  m + ice   ___ ___ ___ ___

3.  n + ice   ___ ___ ___ ___

4.  r + ice   ___ ___ ___ ___

5.  pr + ice   ___ ___ ___ ___ ___

Read these -ice words.

      twice   lice   spice

Complete each sentence. Use the words above.

1. You need to roll the _____ to play.

2. Mia won the game _____ in a row.

3. The _____ of the coat is too high.

Story words to know: roll, highest, pile, lowest
Teacher: Read the story to your students.

Word Family -ice

Name _____

Listen as the story is read to you.
Underline the words in the **-ice** family.
Then read the story to yourself.

Three Nice Mice

Three nice mice.
Three nice mice.

See how they play.
See how they play.

They turn around twice
and roll the dice.

The one who rolls highest
wins a pile of rice.

The one who rolls lowest
has to pay the price.

Three nice mice.
Three nice mice.

Take the story home. Read it to your family.

Name _____

Word Family
-ice

About "Three Nice Mice"

Fill in the circle next to the answer that tells about the story.
Read the parts you circled.

1. Who?
   - ○ two little mice
   - ○ one nice mouse
   - ○ three nice mice

2. What?
   - ○ play a game of dice
   - ○ play tag
   - ○ eat rice

3. Why?
   - ○ to win a slice of pie
   - ○ to win a pile of rice
   - ○ to win a pile of ice

Fill in the circle next to **yes** or **no**.

1. The story tells about real mice.
   - ○ yes   ○ no

2. The mice like to play with dice.
   - ○ yes   ○ no

3. The mice like to eat rice.
   - ○ yes   ○ no

Name _____

Word Family -ice

Write -ice Words

Write the name of each picture.

1. _____ 2. _____ 3. _____

Complete each sentence. Use the words below.

> dice   nice   price   rice   slice

1. Mom cooks the _____ in a pot.

2. We play the game with two _____.

3. Dad put jam on the _____ of bread.

4. You are a _____ friend.

5. Look at the tag to see the _____.

Note: Cut out the slider parts along the dashed lines. Then slip the word strip through the slider window.

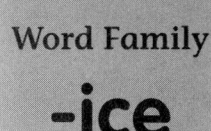

Slide and Read

↑ Pull Up

dice

lice

mice

nice

rice

price

slice

spice

twice

The -ice Family

I know these words! Hooray!

dice   lice   mice

end of
-ice family

price

nice

rice

slice

spice

twice

mice

dice   lice

rice

nice   price

Name _____

Word Family -ide

Meet the -ide Word Family

Word Family Practice

Write the letters on the lines to make **-ide** words.
Then sound out the words you wrote.

1.    h + ide   ___ ___ ___ ___

2.    r + ide   ___ ___ ___ ___

3. 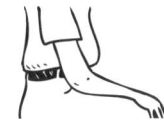   s + ide   ___ ___ ___ ___

4.    w + ide   ___ ___ ___ ___

5.    pr + ide   ___ ___ ___ ___ ___

6.    sl + ide   ___ ___ ___ ___ ___

Complete each sentence. Use the words above.

1. The kitten stays close to its mother's _____.

2. My cat likes to _____ under the couch.

3. A cat can open its mouth very _____.

Story words to know: lion, zoo, hunt, mouth
Teacher: Read the story to your students.

Word Family -ide

Name _____

Listen as the story is read to you.
Underline the words in the **-ide** family.
Then read the story to yourself.

A Pride of Lions

A lion is a very big cat.
Some lions live inside a zoo.
Most lions live outside.

They hunt for food.
A lion opens its mouth very wide.
It takes big bites.

The fur of a lion is yellow-brown.
The color helps a lion hide in dry grass.

Some lions live together.
They are called a pride.

A baby lion stays near its mother's side.
She keeps the cub safe.

Take the story home. Read it to your family.

Name _____

Word Family
-ide

About "A Pride of Lions"

Fill in the circle next to the correct answer. Write the word on the line.

1. Some lions live inside a _____.

   ○ zoo
   ○ house
   ○ grass

2. When lions live together, they are called a _____.

   ○ hide
   ○ bride
   ○ pride

3. A baby lion is called a _____.

   ○ kitten
   ○ cub
   ○ puppy

Draw a line to make a match.

1.   •   • A cub stays by its mother's side.

2.    •   • A lion can hide in dry grass.

3.    •   • A lion can open its mouth wide.

© Evan-Moor Corp. • EMC 3355 • Word Family Stories and Activities

Name _____

Word Family -ide

Write **-ide** Words

Complete each sentence. Use the words below.

> hide   inside   ride   side   slide

1. I like to _____ my bike.

2. My dog likes to _____ his bone.

3. Do you like to play _____ or outside?

4. The ice makes me slip and _____.

5. The cub is at its mother's _____.

Write a sentence about a park. Use the word **slide**.

_____

_____

Write a sentence about a bus. Use the word **ride**.

_____

_____

Note: Cut out the slider parts along the dashed lines.
Then slip the word strip through the slider window.

Word Family -ide

Slide and Read

Pull Up

hide

ride

side

tide

wide

bride

pride

slide

inside

outside

The -ide Family

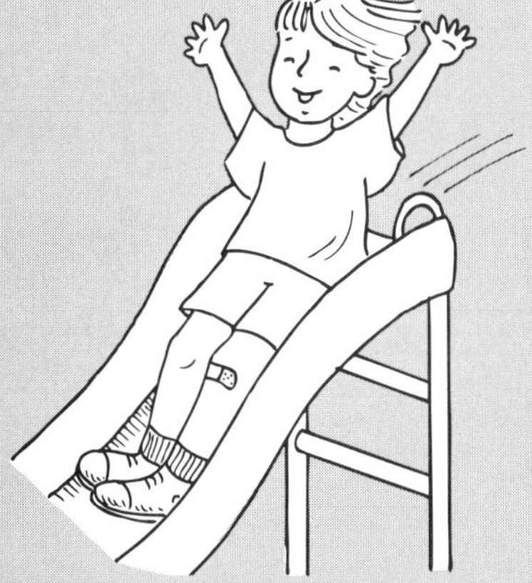

I know these words!

Hooray!

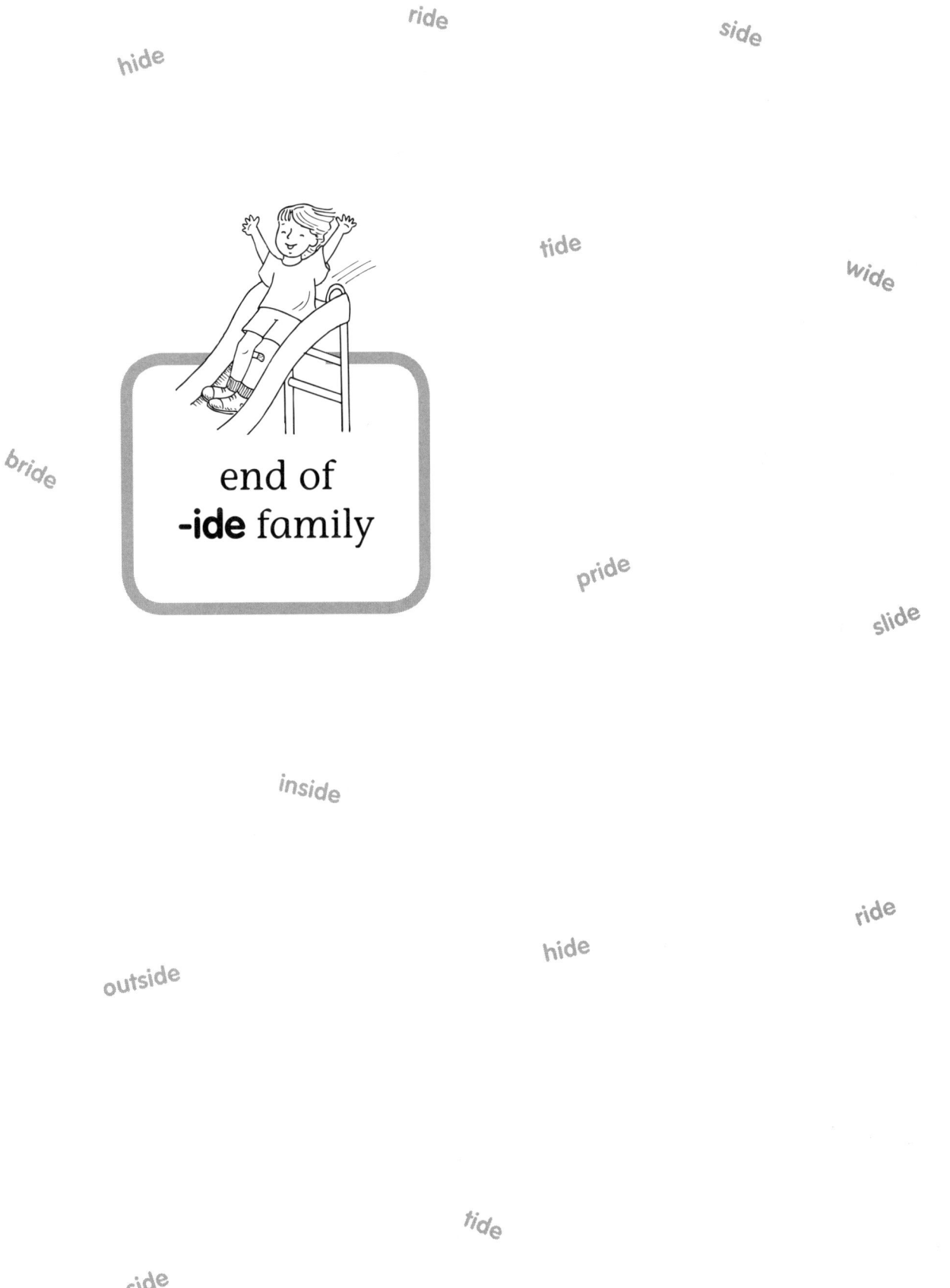

Name _____

Word Family
-ine

Meet the **-ine** Word Family

Word Family Practice

Write the letters on the lines to make **-ine** words.
Then sound out the words you wrote.

1.  l + ine   ___ ___ ___ ___

2.  m + ine   ___ ___ ___ ___

3.  n + ine   ___ ___ ___ ___

4.  p + ine   ___ ___ ___ ___

5.  sh + ine   ___ ___ ___ ___ ___

6.  wh + ine   ___ ___ ___ ___ ___

Complete each sentence. Use the words above.

1. We stand in _____ to get on the school bus.

2. My brother will _____ to get his way.

3. When will the rain stop so the sun can _____?

Story words to know: trip, shook, number, first
Teacher: Read the story to your students.

Word Family -ine

Name _____

Listen as the story is read to you.
Underline the words in the **-ine** family.
Then read the story to yourself.

Sam Feels Fine

Sam woke up.

He saw the sun shine into his room.

Sam said, "Can I go on the school trip?"

Mom shook her head.

"You're sick," said Mom.

Sam began to whine.

"But I feel fine.

All the kids are going."

Mom gave in.

The kids got in line for the bus.

Sam was number nine in line.

Leo got on first.

"The seat by you is mine," said Sam.

They had a great time.

Take the story home. Read it to your family.

Word Family -ine

About "Sam Feels Fine"

Fill in the circle next to **yes** or **no**.

1. Sam saw the rain from his room.

    ○ yes   ○ no

2. Sam whines to get his way.

    ○ yes   ○ no

3. Sam goes on a school trip.

    ○ yes   ○ no

4. Leo is number nine in line.

    ○ yes   ○ no

5. Sam and Tim sit together.

    ○ yes   ○ no

Show when each thing happened. Write **1**, **2**, **3**, **4**.

_____ The sun shines.

_____ Sam says, "The seat by you is mine!"

_____ Sam is number nine in line.

_____ Sam whines to his mom.

Name _____

Word Family
-ine

Write **-ine** Words

Fill in the circle next to the name of each picture.

1.

    ○ like
    ○ live
    ○ line

2.

    ○ mine
    ○ pine
    ○ shine

3.

    ○ whine
    ○ fine
    ○ nine

Complete each sentence. Use the words below.

> line   mine   pine   shine   spine

1. I see the stars _____.

2. That green coat is _____.

3. The bones in your back are your _____.

4. A _____ tree has cones.

5. The kids stand in _____ for the bus.

72   Word Family Stories and Activities • EMC 3355 • © Evan-Moor Corp.

Note: Cut out the slider parts along the dashed lines.
Then slip the word strip through the slider window.

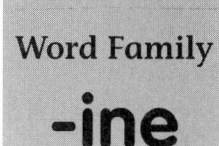

Slide and Read

↑ Pull Up

fine
line
mine
nine
pine
vine
wine
shine
spine
twine
whine

The -ine Family

I know these words!

Hooray!

fine · line · mine · nine · pine · vine · wine · shine · spine · twine · whine · fine · mine · line · nine

end of -ine family

Name _____

Word Family -oke

Meet the -oke Word Family

Word Family Practice

Write the letters on the lines to make **-oke** words.
Then sound out the words you wrote.

1.  j + oke   __ __ __ __

2.  p + oke   __ __ __ __

3.  w + oke   __ __ __ __

4.  br + oke   __ __ __ __ __

5.  sm + oke   __ __ __ __ __

Read these **-oke** words.

      spoke   choke   stroke

Complete each sentence. Use the words above.

1. She _____ up to the smell of _____.

2. The man _____ on his cell phone every day.

3. The heater _____, so now we are cold.

Story words to know: smell, heater, phone, quickly, hold
Teacher: Read the story to your students.

Word Family -oke

Name _____

Listen as the story is read to you.
Underline the words in the **-oke** family.
Then read the story to yourself.

Smoke

Rosa gave her mom a poke.

"What is it?" asked Mom.

"I smell smoke!" said Rosa.

Mom woke fast.

"It looks like the heater broke," she said.

"Where there's smoke, there's fire.

I have to call for help."

Mom took her phone.

She spoke quickly.

"Hold my hand, Rosa.

Let's go as fast as we can."

Take the story home. Read it to your family.

Name _____

Word Family
-oke

About "Smoke"

Fill in the circle next to the correct answer.

1. What is the story about?

    ○ Rosa makes a joke.
    ○ Rosa smells smoke.
    ○ Mom gives Rosa a poke.

2. Why will Mom call for help?

    ○ There is a bear.
    ○ There is rain.
    ○ There is smoke.

3. Why is there smoke?

    ○ The car broke.
    ○ A dish broke.
    ○ The heater broke.

4. What tells that there is a fire?

    ○ smoke
    ○ snow
    ○ logs

Show when each thing happened. Write **1**, **2**, **3**.

_____ Mom woke fast.

_____ Mom and Rosa go.

_____ Rosa gives Mom a poke.

© Evan-Moor Corp. • EMC 3355 • Word Family Stories and Activities

Name _____

Word Family -oke

Write -oke Words

Fill in the circle next to the name of each picture.

1.
   - ○ smoke
   - ○ spoke
   - ○ smell

2.
   - ○ poke
   - ○ woke
   - ○ pole

3.
   - ○ choke
   - ○ joke
   - ○ broke

Complete each sentence. Use the words below.

> joke   poke   smoke   spoke   woke

1. I _____ up late.

2. Fire makes _____.

3. Fran likes to _____ me.

4. I know a funny _____.

5. Rosa _____ on the phone.

Note: Cut out the slider parts along the dashed lines. Then slip the word strip through the slider window.

Word Family -oke

Slide and Read

↑ Pull Up

joke

poke

woke

broke

choke

smoke

spoke

stroke

The **-oke** Family

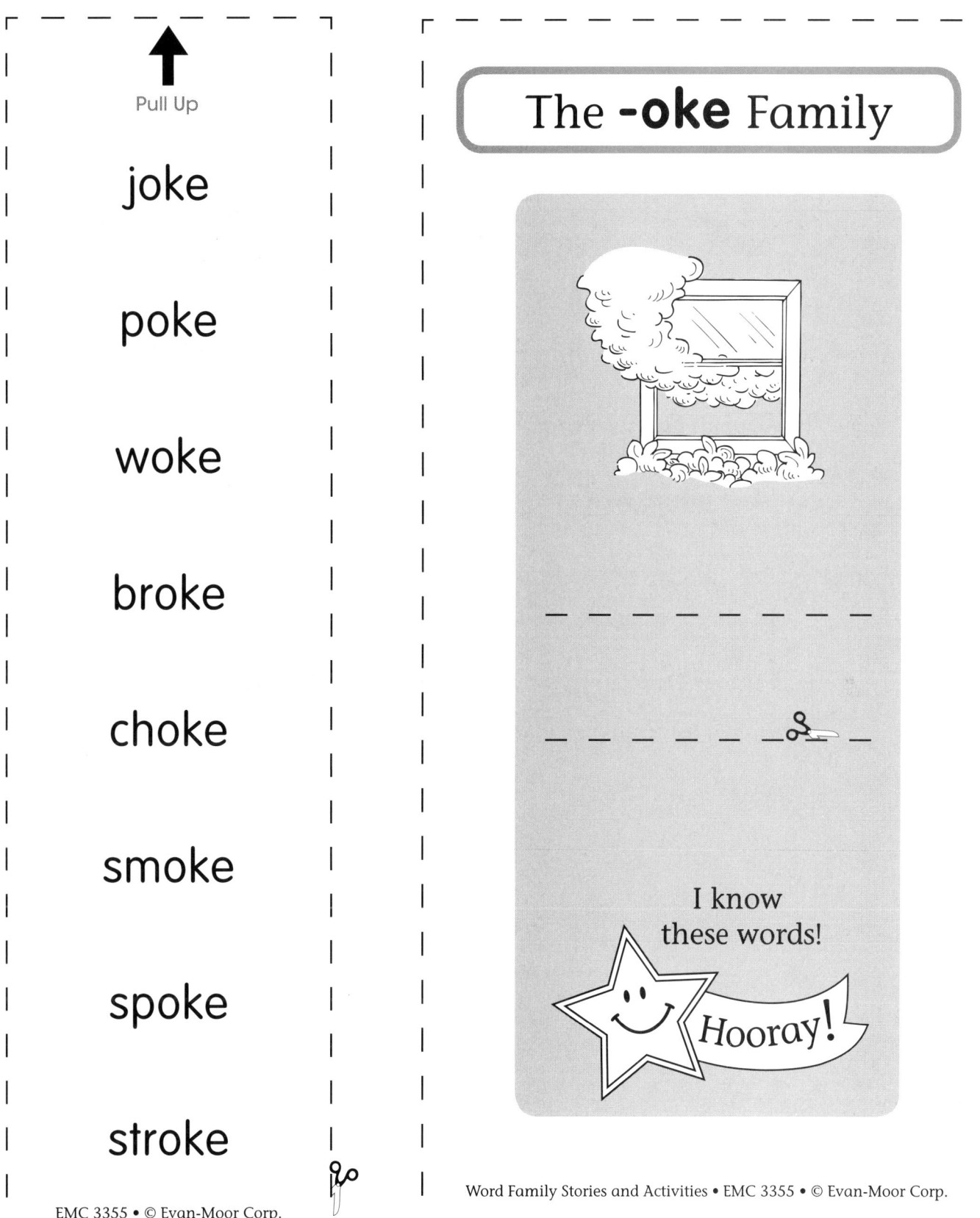

I know these words! Hooray!

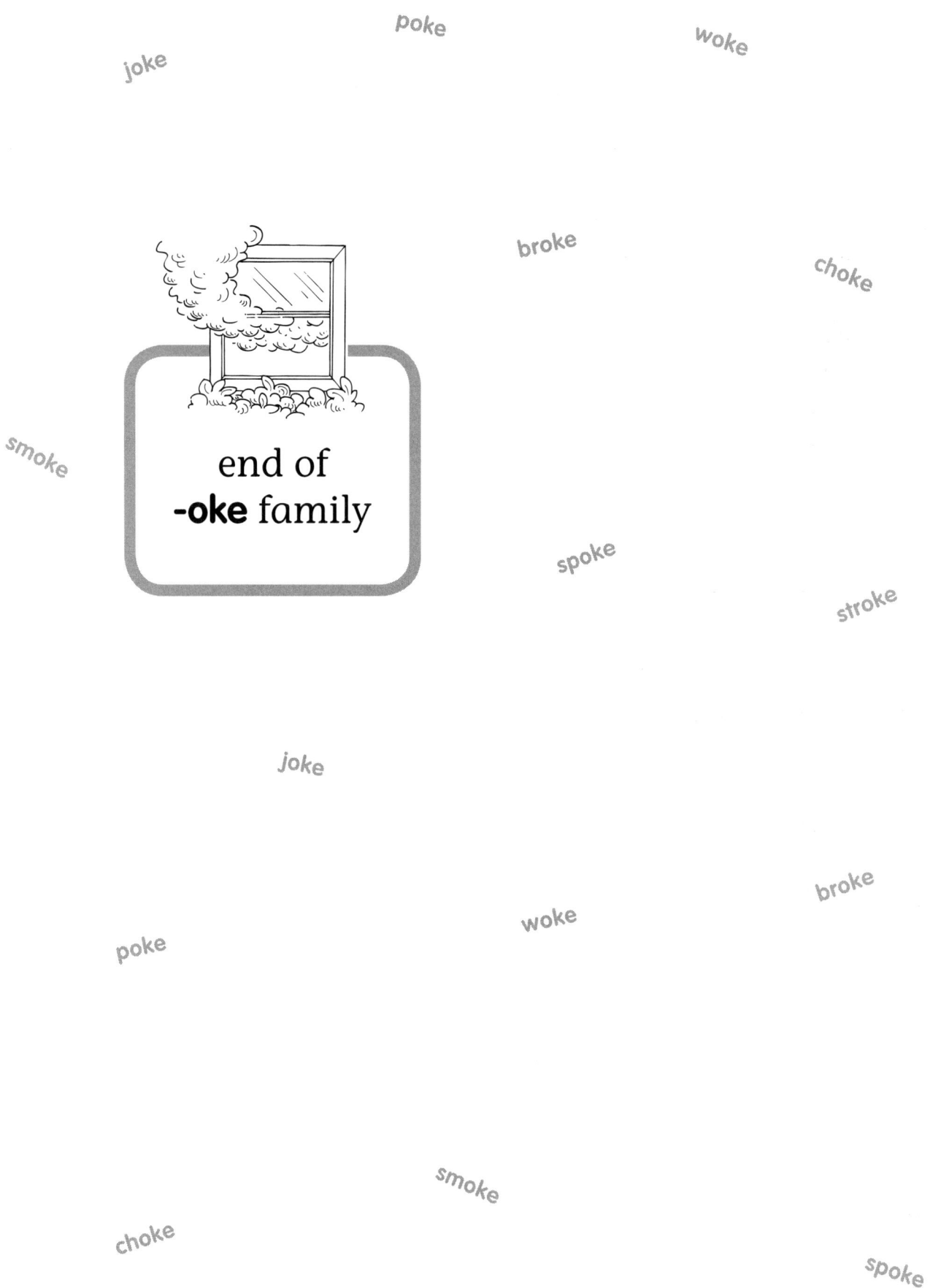

Name _____

Word Family -old

Meet the -old Word Family

Word Family Practice

Write the letters on the lines to make **-old** words.
Then sound out the words you wrote.

1.    c + old   ___ ___ ___ ___

2.    g + old   ___ ___ ___ ___

3.    h + old   ___ ___ ___ ___

4.    t + old   ___ ___ ___ ___

5.    sc + old   ___ ___ ___ ___ ___

Read these **-old** words.

        bold   mold   fold

Complete each sentence. Use the words above.

1. I _____ my puppy when he chews on my shoe.

2. The puppy likes to splash in _____ water.

3. My puppy is the color of _____.

Story words to know: wrong, should, splash, afraid
Teacher: Read the story to your students.

Word Family -old

Name_____

Listen as the story is read to you.
Underline the words in the **-old** family.
Then read the story to yourself.

What Can It Be?

One thing is wrong with my puppy.
She does not have a name.

Her fur is gold.
I can call her Sunny.

She likes when I hold her.
Should I call her Hugs?

I scold her when she bites.
Is Jaws a good name?

She likes cold water.
I can call her Splash.

She is bold and not afraid.
Should I call her Brave?

Can you think of a good name?

Take the story home. Read it to your family.

Name _____

Word Family
-old

About "What Can It Be?"

Fill in the circle next to the correct answer.

1. What is wrong with the puppy?

    ○ She is sick.
    ○ She is old.
    ○ She needs a name.

2. Why is Jaws a good name?

    ○ The puppy likes to bite.
    ○ The puppy has gold fur.
    ○ The puppy likes to play.

3. What does it mean to be **bold**?

    ○ to be big
    ○ to be little
    ○ to be brave

Draw a line to tell why the name is good.

1. Brave   •   • The puppy has gold fur.

2. Splash   •   • The puppy is bold.

3. Sunny   •   • The puppy likes cold water.

Name _____

Word Family -old

Write -old Words

Fill in the circle next to the name of each picture.

1.
   - ○ sold
   - ○ scold
   - ○ sun

2.
   - ○ cat
   - ○ hold
   - ○ cold

3.
   - ○ go
   - ○ gold
   - ○ game

Complete each sentence. Use the words below.

> bold   cold   hold   sold   told

1. I will _____ Dad's hand.

2. The teacher _____ me to sit down in my chair.

3. The ice feels _____.

4. Mom _____ our old car.

5. Lee saved a baby. He is _____.

84   Word Family Stories and Activities • EMC 3355 • © Evan-Moor Corp.

Note: Cut out the slider parts along the dashed lines.
Then slip the word strip through the slider window.

Word Family
-old

Slide and Read

↑
Pull Up

bold

cold

fold

gold

hold

mold

sold

told

scold

The **-old** Family

I know these words!

Hooray!

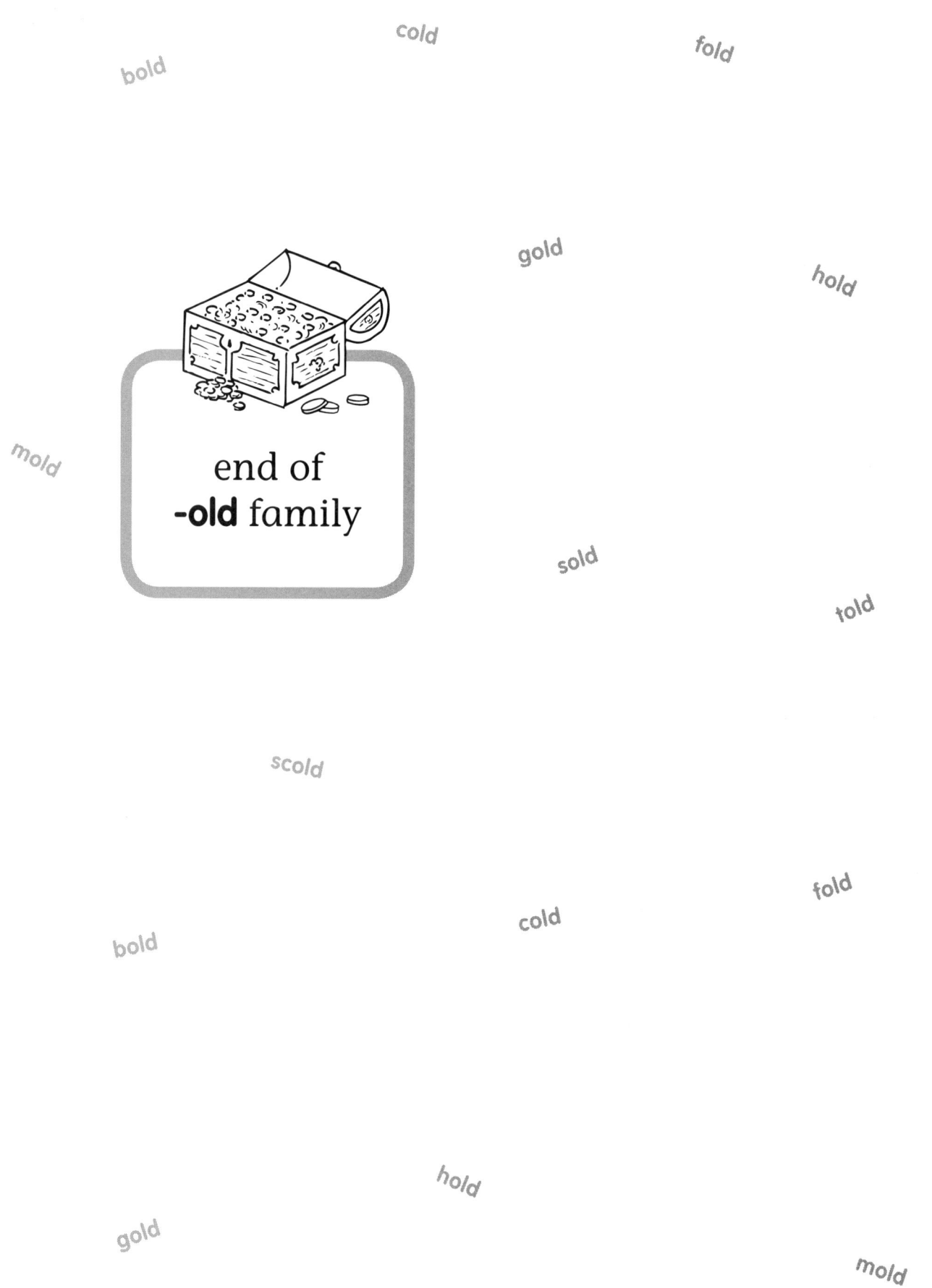

Name _____

Word Family -ow

Meet the -ow Word Family

Word Family Practice

Write the letters on the lines to make -ow words.
Then sound out the words you wrote.

1.  r + ow ___ ___ ___

2.  t + ow ___ ___ ___

3.  m + ow ___ ___ ___

4.  gr + ow ___ ___ ___ ___

5.  sl + ow ___ ___ ___ ___

6.  kn + ow ___ ___ ___ ___

Complete each sentence. Use the words above.

1. Please _____ the grass in the yard.

2. Do you _____ my sister Sally?

3. _____, _____, _____ your boat.

Story words to know: stuck, boat, pond
Teacher: Read the story to your students.

Word Family -ow

Name _____

Listen as the story is read to you.
Underline the words in the **-ow** family.
Then read the story to yourself.

I Know

Our car is stuck in the snow.
I know we need a tow.

Our grass will grow and grow.
I know it needs a mow.

Our boat is in the pond.
I know we need to row.

We need a tow,
We need to mow,
We need to row.

I know, I know!

Take the story home. Read it to your family.

Name _____

Word Family -ow

About "I Know"

Fill in the circle next to the correct answer.

1. First?

   ○ car needs a tow
   ○ boat needs a row
   ○ grass needs a mow

2. Next?

   ○ car needs a tow
   ○ boat needs a row
   ○ grass needs a mow

3. Last?

   ○ car needs a tow
   ○ boat needs a row
   ○ grass needs a mow

Draw a line to make a match.

1. car   • will grow and grow

2. boat   • stuck in the snow

3. grass   • in the pond

Write -ow Words

Word Family -OW

Fill in the circle next to the name of each picture.

1.
   ○ blow
   ○ black
   ○ bow

2.
   ○ slow
   ○ crow
   ○ glow

3.
   ○ row
   ○ rope
   ○ rose

Complete each sentence. Use the words below.

> blow   grow   know   show   slow

1. Do you _____ how to tell time?

2. The plant will _____ tall if you feed it.

3. Bill likes to _____ bubbles with his gum.

4. Mom can _____ you how to skate.

5. A snail is a _____ animal.

Note: Cut out the slider parts along the dashed lines.
Then slip the word strip through the slider window.

Word Family -ow

Slide and Read

↑ Pull Up

bow

mow

row

tow

blow

crow

glow

grow

know

slow

snow

The -ow Family

I know these words!

Hooray!

end of -ow family

bow
mow
row
tow
blow
crow
glow
grow
know
slow
snow
bow
row
mow
tow

Name _____

Word Family -y

Meet the -y Word Family

Word Family Practice

Write the letters on the lines to make -y words.
Then sound out the words you wrote.

1.    fl + y   ___ ___ ___

2.    sk + y   ___ ___ ___

3.    sh + y   ___ ___ ___

4.    sp + y   ___ ___ ___

5.    wh + y   ___ ___ ___

Read these -y words.

      try   fry   butterfly

Complete each sentence. Use the words above.

1. _____ did you _____ to kick me?

2. I see a plane flying in the _____.

3. Pat likes to _____ on his older sister.

Story words to know: wings, something, high, June
Teacher: Read the story to your students.

Word Family

-y

Name _____

Listen as the story is read to you.
Underline the words in the **-y** family.
Then read the story to yourself.

I Spy

I spy with my little eye,
   a bug with four big wings.
Oh me, oh my!
I see a butterfly.

I spy with my little eye,
   something blue way up high.
Oh me, oh my!
I see a butterfly in the sky.

I spy with my little eye,
   what comes after June.
Oh me, oh my!
I see a butterfly in the sky in July.

Now you try.

Take the story home. Read it to your family.

Name _____

Word Family
-y

About "I Spy"

Fill in the circle next to the correct answer.

1. What does it mean to **spy**?

    ○ to watch
    ○ to cry
    ○ to want

2. Where is the butterfly?

    ○ on a wall
    ○ under a bush
    ○ in the sky

3. What comes next? May, June, _____

    ○ March
    ○ July
    ○ Sunday

4. What is blue and way up high?

    ○ the sun
    ○ the plane
    ○ the sky

5. What is the story about?

    ○ playing the "I Spy" game
    ○ helping Dad
    ○ raking the grass

Name _____

Word Family -y

Write -y Words

Complete each sentence. Use the words below.

> cry   dry   fly   sky   try

1. Always _____ to do your best.

2. Meg will _____ the wet plate.

3. Stars filled the night _____.

4. A _____ is a bug with two wings.

5. I am sad to see you _____.

Write sentences.

Ask a question. Use the word **why**.

Why _____

_____?

Tell about something you have. Use the word **my**.

My _____

_____.

Note: Cut out the slider parts along the dashed lines. Then slip the word strip through the slider window.

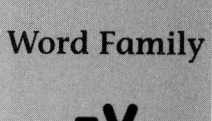

Slide and Read

↑ Pull Up

cry

dry

fly

fry

shy

sky

spy

try

why

July

butterfly

The -y Family

I know these words!

Hooray!

end of -y family

cry dry fly

fry sky

shy

spy

try

why

butterfly cry

July

fly

dry fry

Answer Key

Page 3

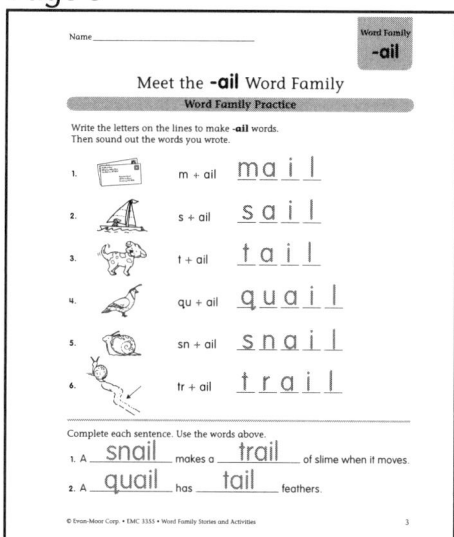

Page 4

Page 5

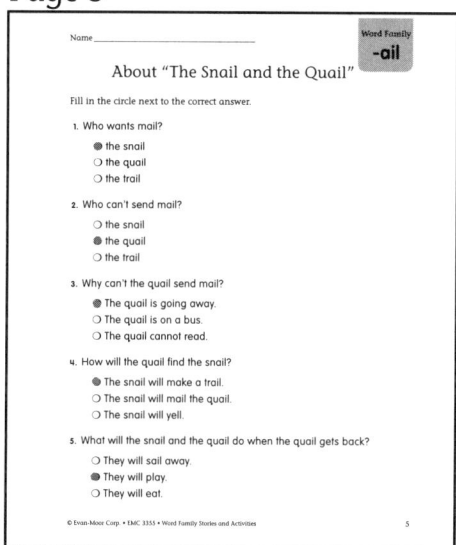

Page 6

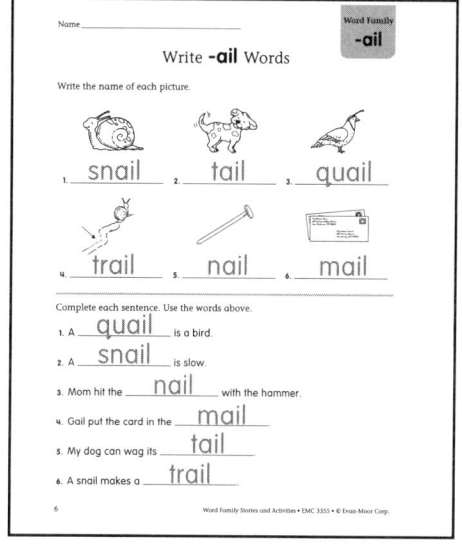

Page 9

Page 10

Page 11
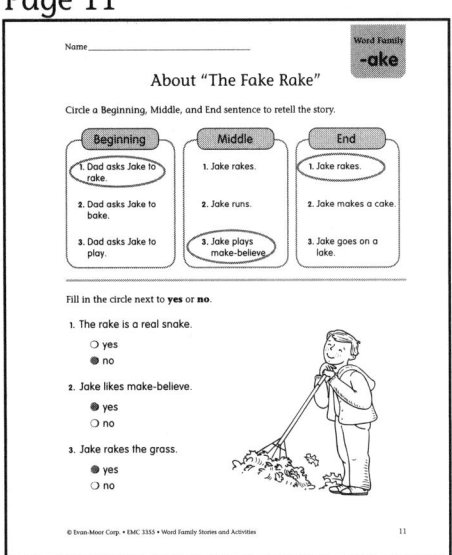

Page 12
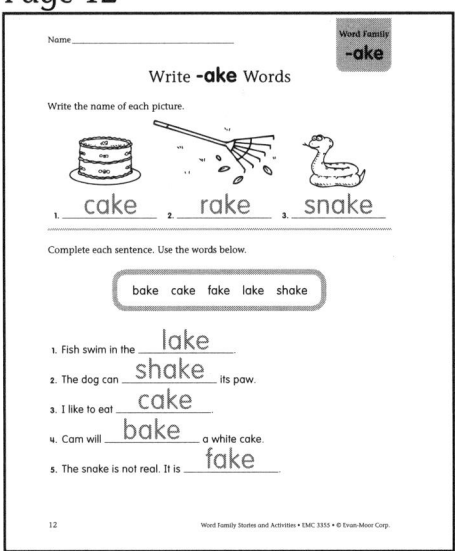

Page 15
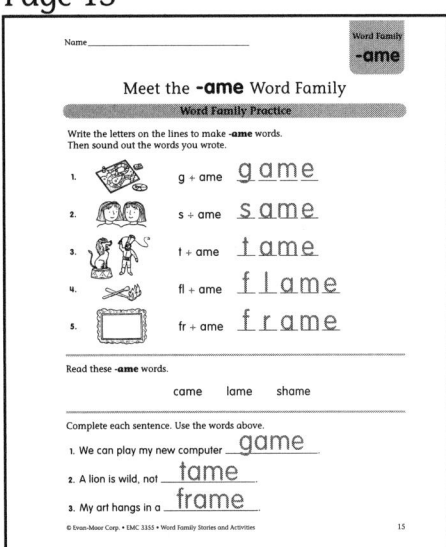

Page 16

Page 17
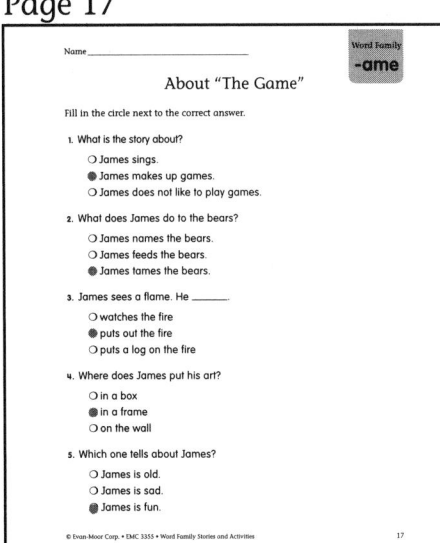

Page 18
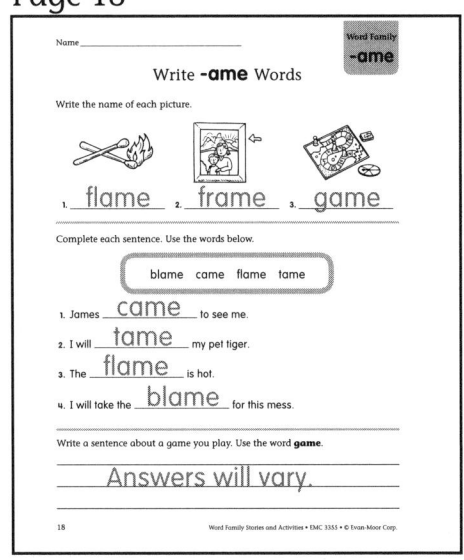

Page 21
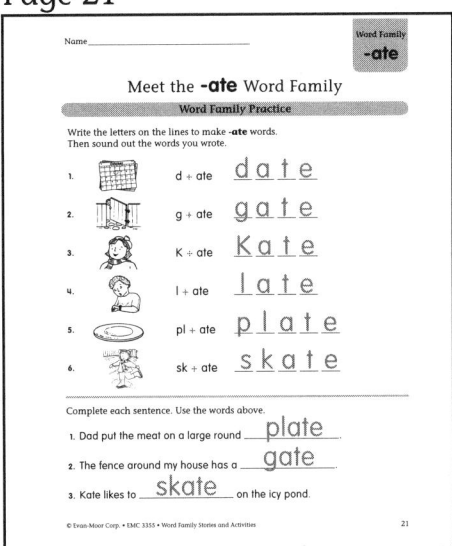

Page 22

Page 23
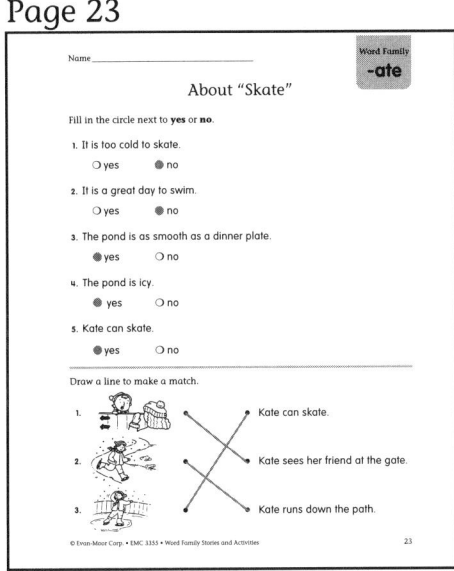

Page 24
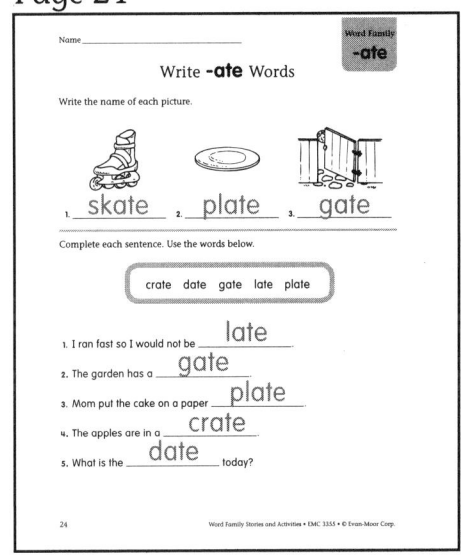

Page 27
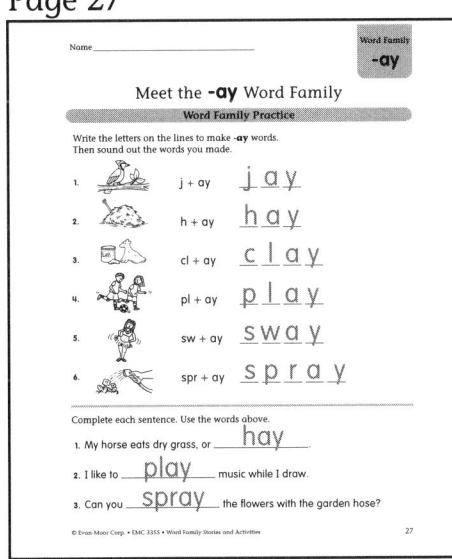

Page 28

Page 29
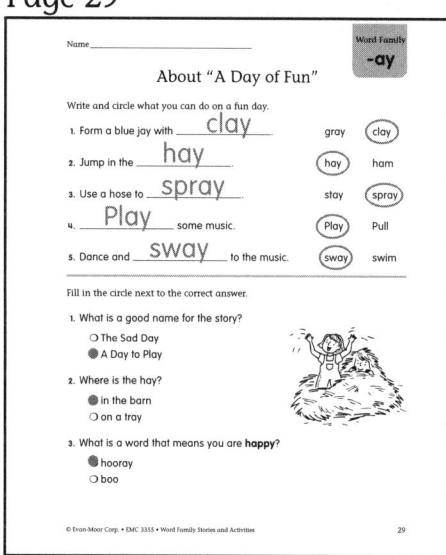

Page 30
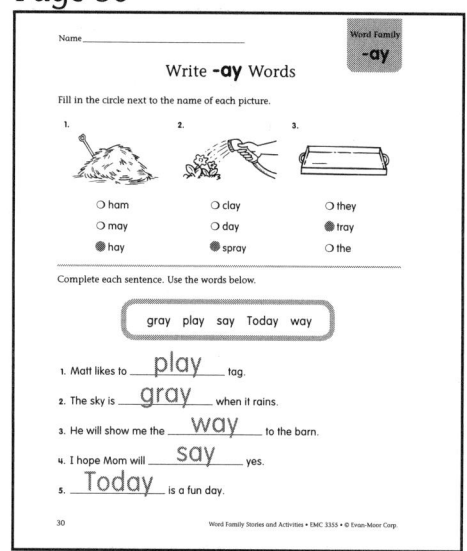

Page 33
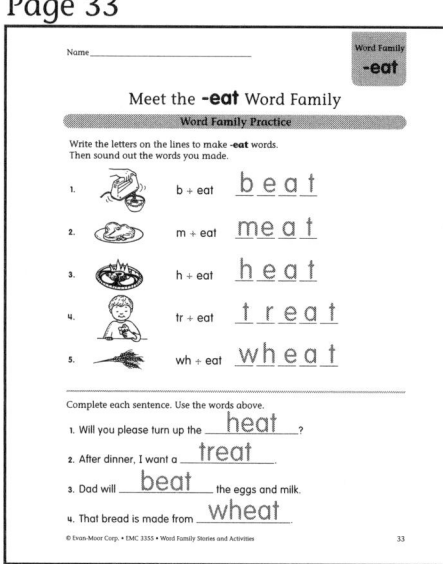

Page 34

Page 35
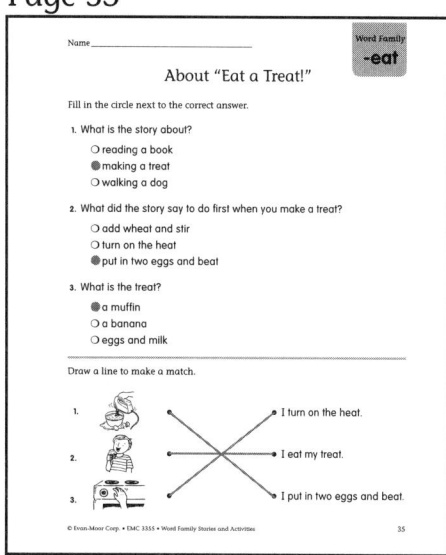

Page 36
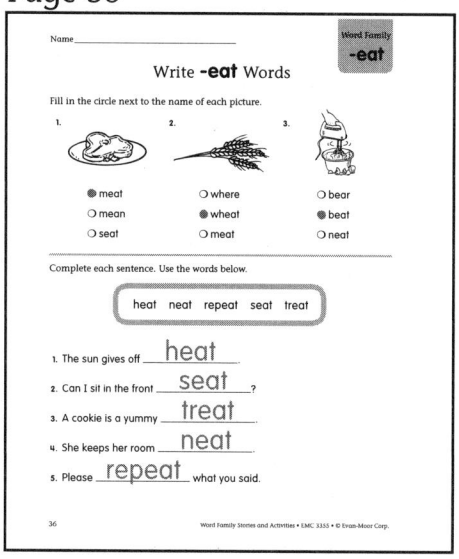

Page 39
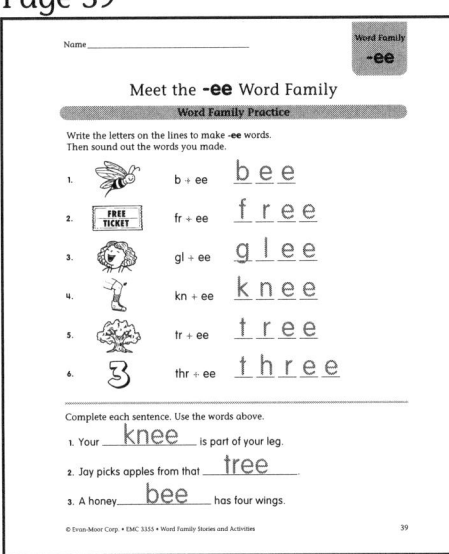

Page 40

Page 41
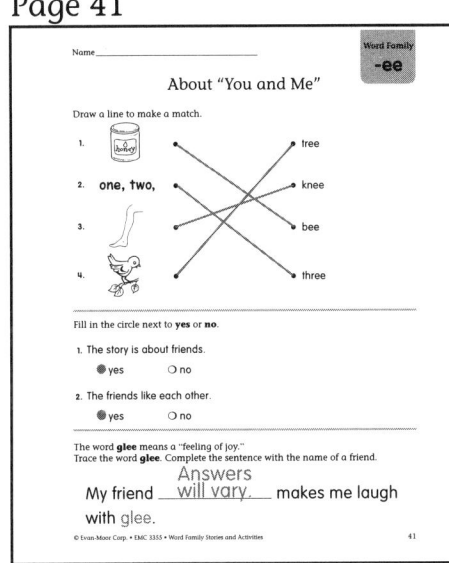

Page 42
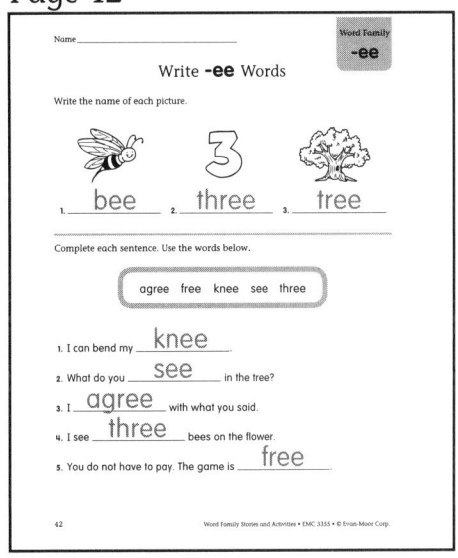

Page 45
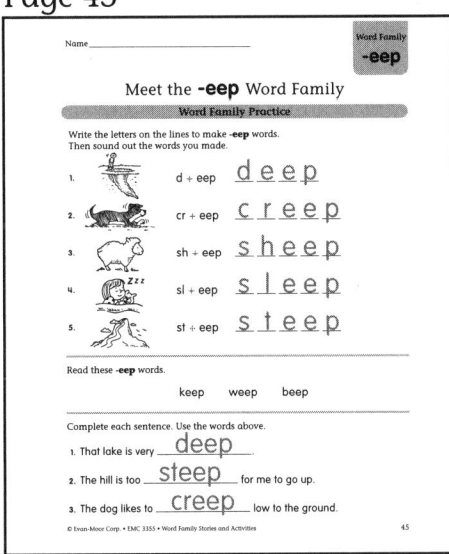

Page 46

Page 47
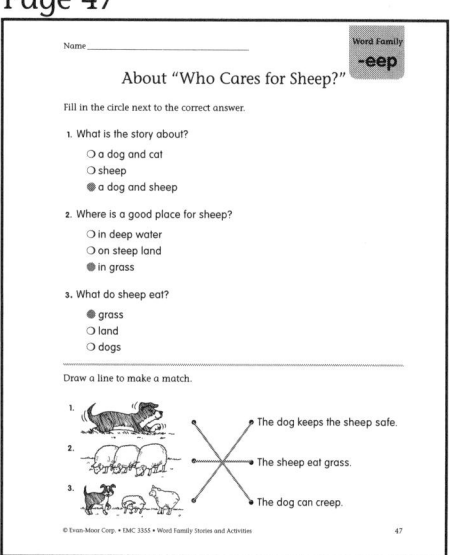

Page 48

Page 51
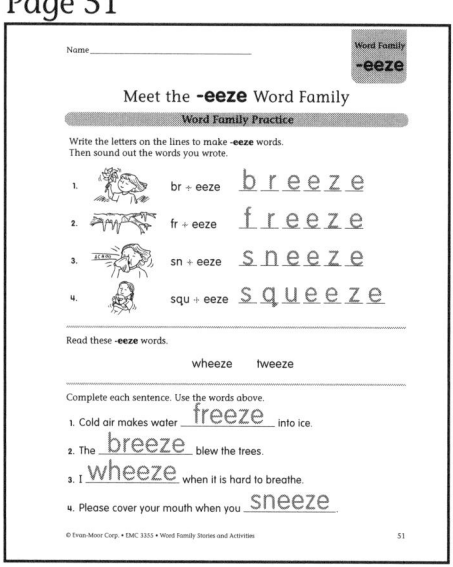

Page 52
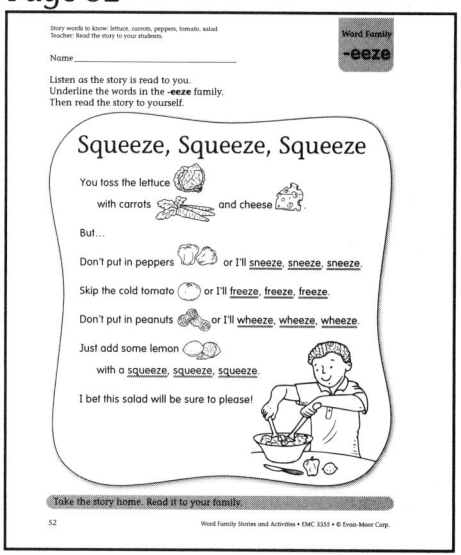

Page 53
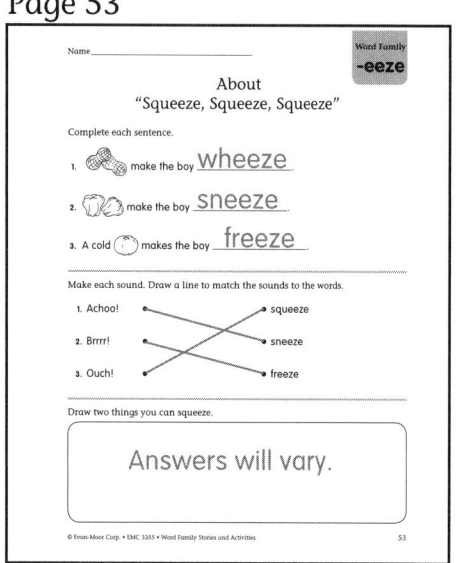

Page 54
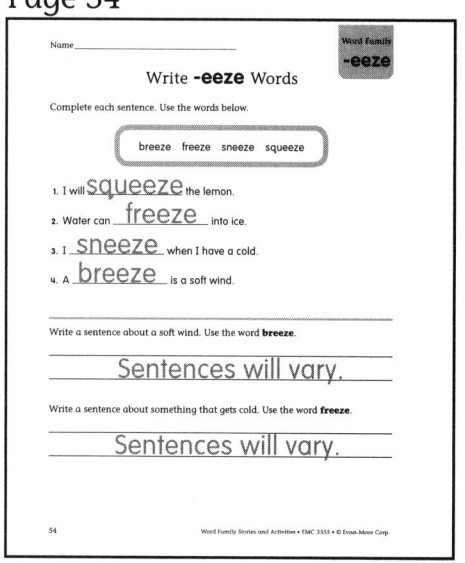

Page 57
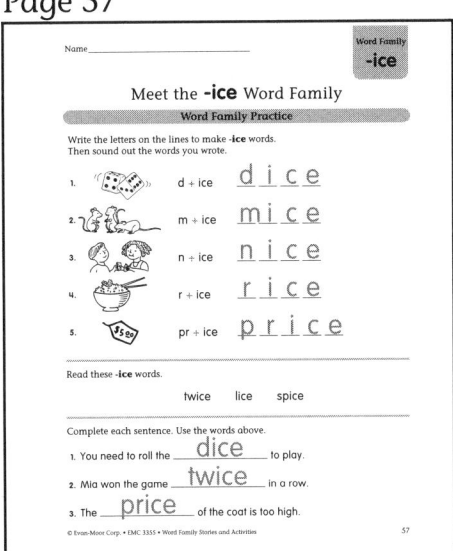

Page 58

Page 59
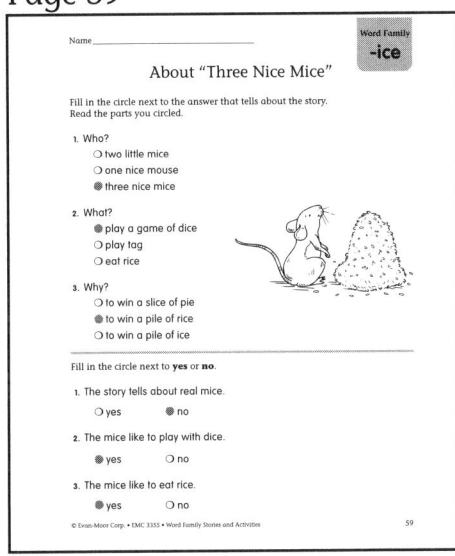

Page 60
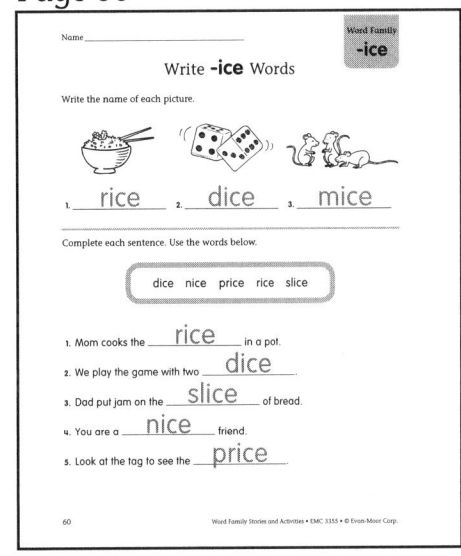

Page 63
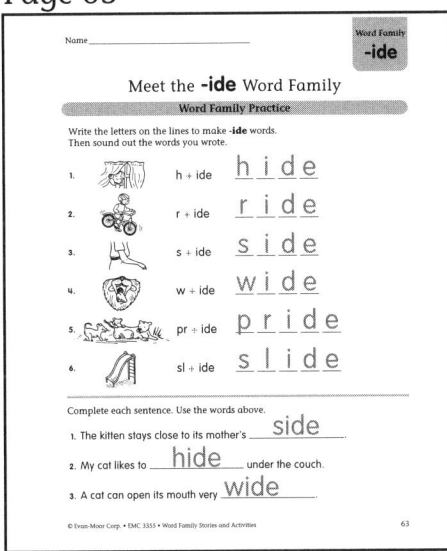

Page 64

Page 65
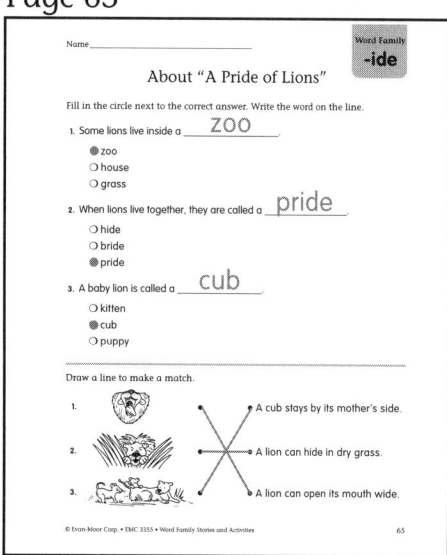

Page 66
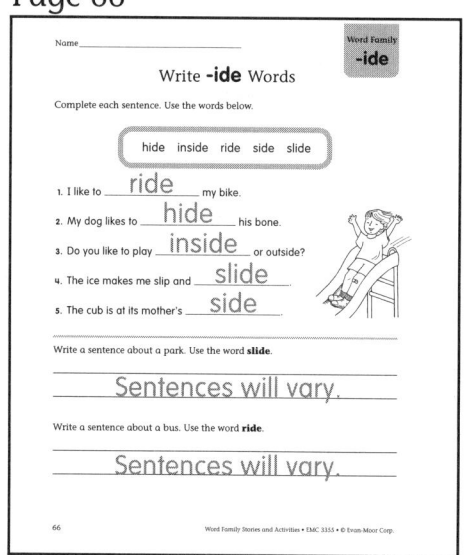

Page 69
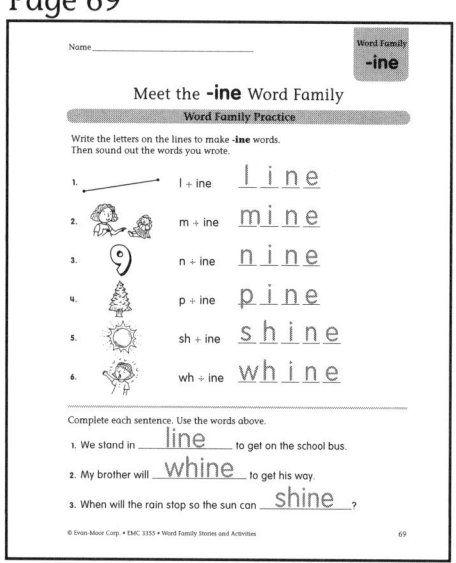

Page 70

Page 71
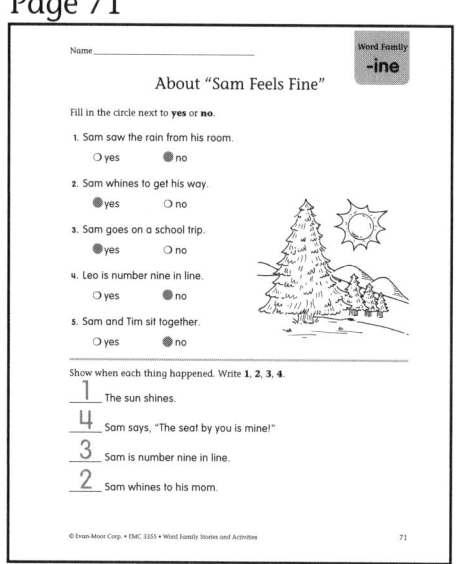

Page 72
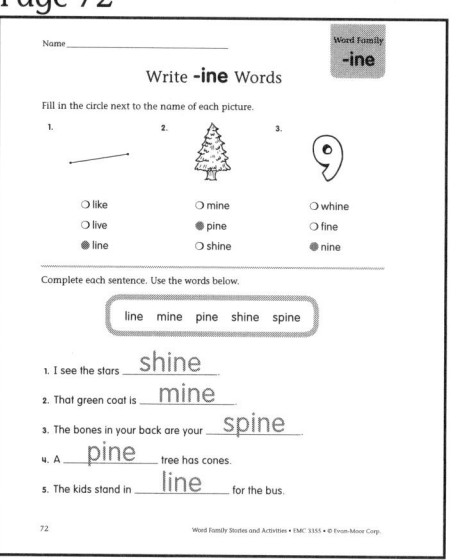

Page 75
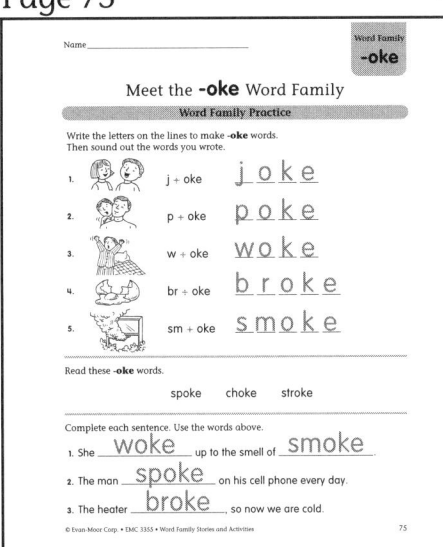

Page 76

Page 77

Page 78
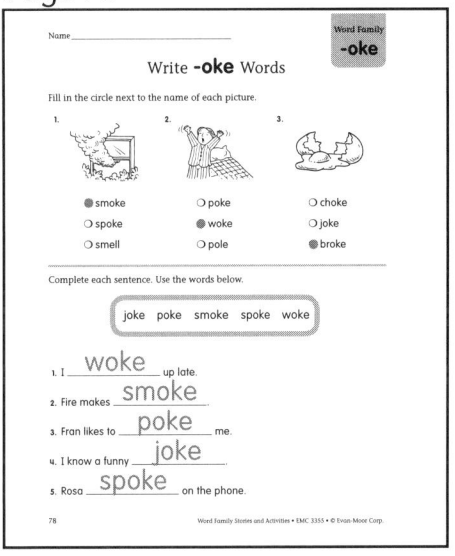

Page 81
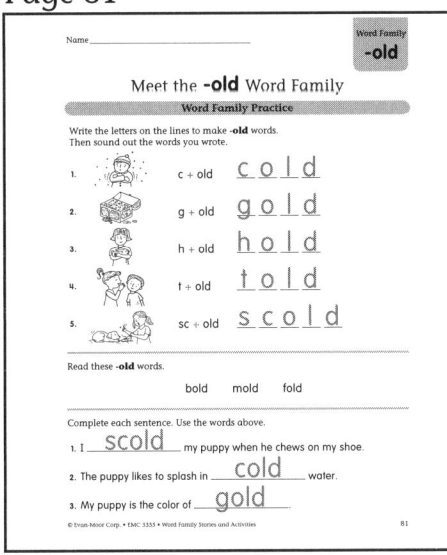

Page 82

Page 83
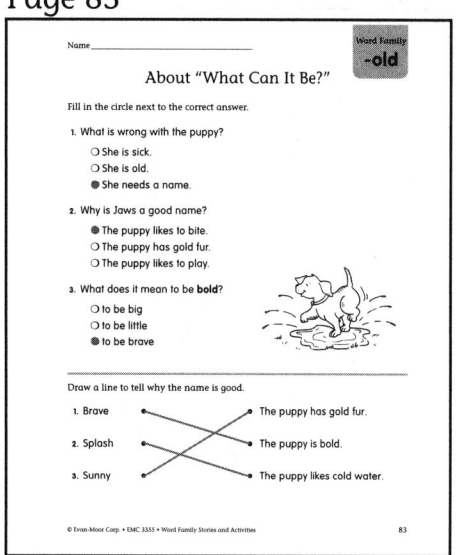

Page 84
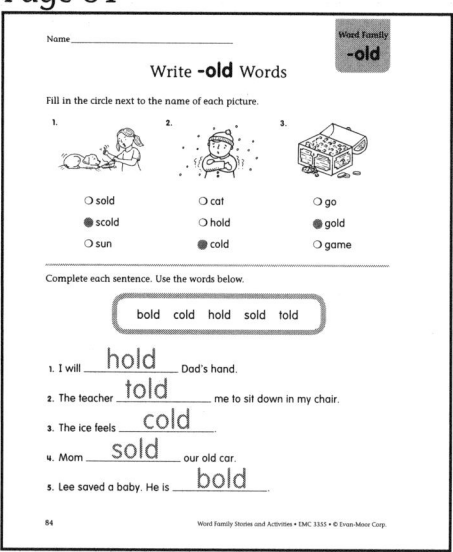

Page 87
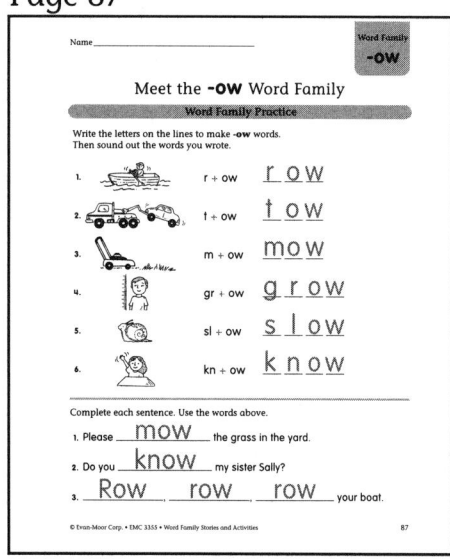

Page 88

Page 89
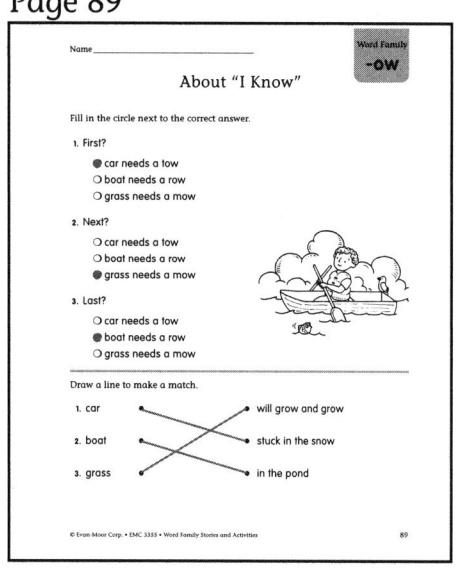

Page 90
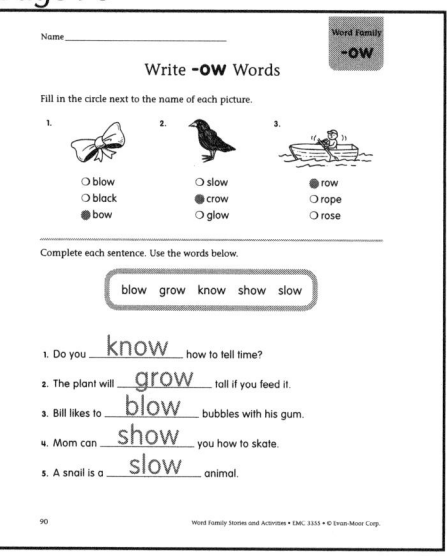

Page 93
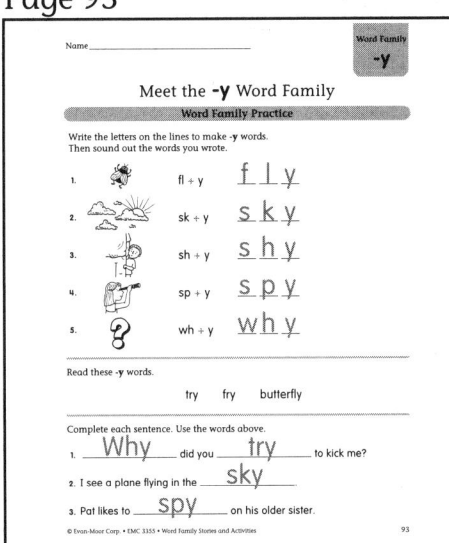

Page 94

Page 95
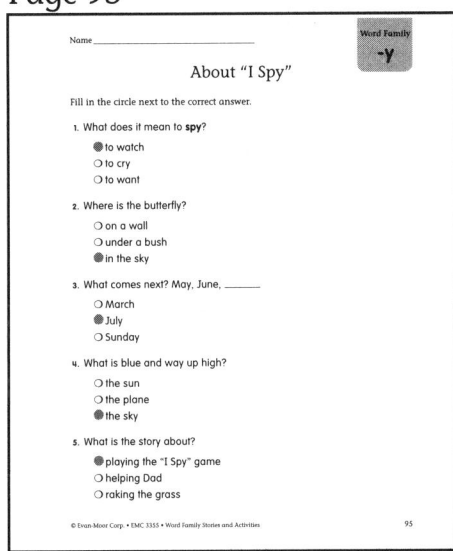

Page 96
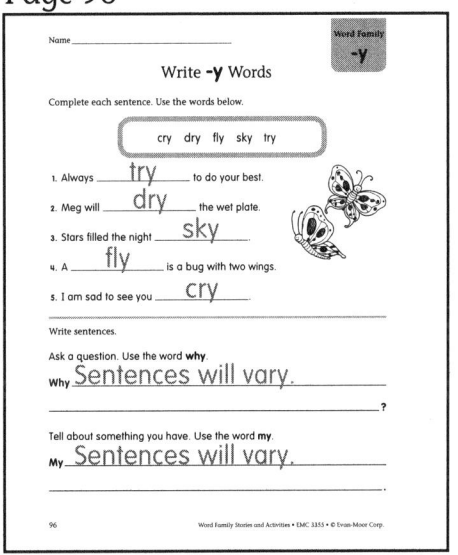

Bulletin Board

Use the train template to make a word family train for your bulletin board.

Write the word family on the engine of the train and word family words on the boxcars. Reproduce as many boxcars as needed to complete the word family your class has mastered.

112 Word Family Stories and Activities • EMC 3355 • © Evan-Moor Corp.